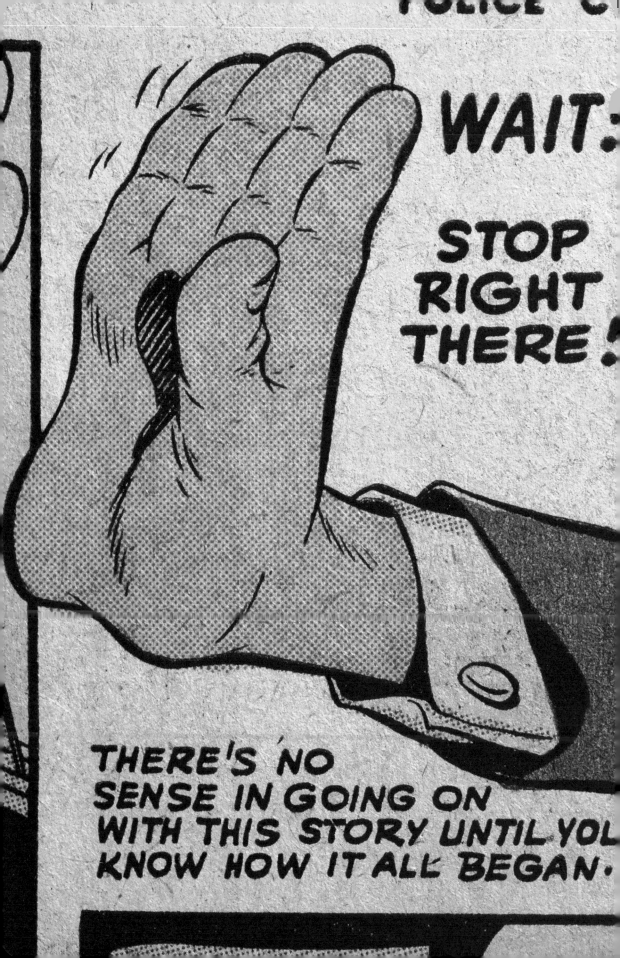

10¢

A VITAL BOOK

PLASTIC MAN

in

The Gay Nineties Nightmare!

FOUR BIG PLASTIC MAN STORIES... Packed with *Thrills, Chills* and *LAFFS!*

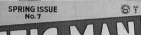

—JACK COLE

SEPTEMBER
No. 19

PLASTIC MAN

10¢

PULVERIZES A PREHISTORIC PLUNDERER!

No. 4

PLASTIC MA

LAUGHS GALORE *with* PLASTIC MAN and his pal WOOZY!

SPRING ISSUE
No. 7

PLASTIC MAN

10¢

LIGHTNING RODS FOR SALE!

WINTER ISSUE
No. 10

PLASTIC MAN

10¢

LINES UP AGAINST CRIME!

SEPTEMBER
No. 13

PLASTIC MA

GAMBLES *against* **DEATH** *with* MR. HAZARD!

TOMATOES

10¢

A VITAL BOOK

PLASTIC MAN

IN THE
Game of Death!

4 Full Length PLASTIC MAN Picture Stories!

HE ST-R-E-T-C-H-E-S, SHRINKS AND BENDS!!

PLASTIC MAN

10¢

BRINGS YOU THRILLS—

WOOZY, THE LAUGHS!

NO. 5

PLASTIC MA

PLASTIC MAN and WOOZY bring you new Laughs and Thrills!

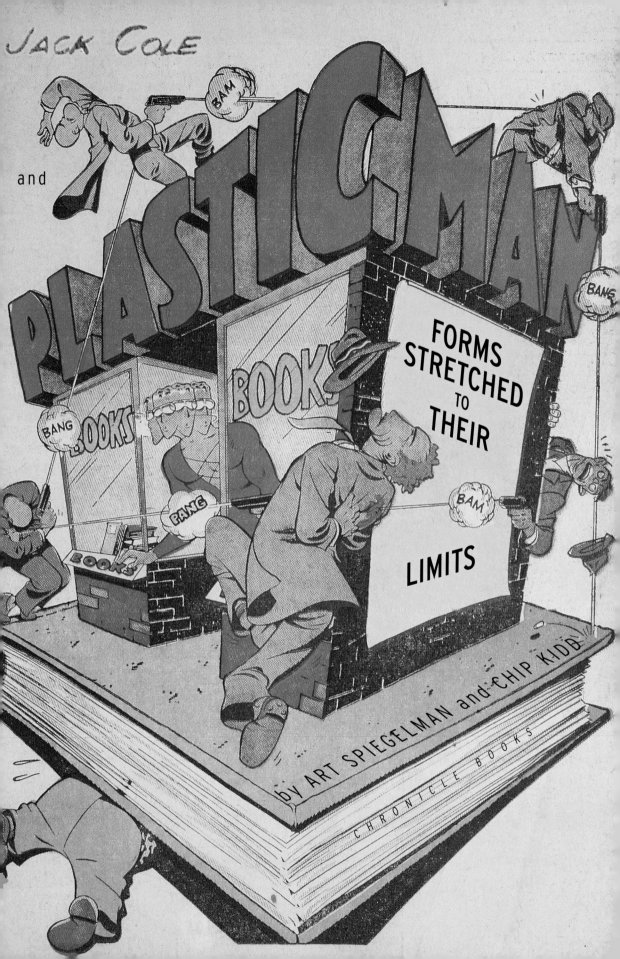

Library of Congress
Cataloging-in-Publication Data is available
ISBN 0-8118-3179-5

Printed in China
10 9 8 7 6 5 4 3 2 1

DESIGN ASSISTANCE BY CHIN-YEE LAI

Photographs by Marc Witz
Digital restoration by Madeleine Blaustein

Grateful acknowledgment is made to *The New Yorker*, where the text originally appeared, in slightly different form, as "Forms Stretched to Their Limits" (April 19, 1999); and to *Playboy* magazine for permission to reproduce artwork by Jack Cole on pages 113–27—copyright © 1954, 1955, 1956, 1957, 1958, 1959, 1982, 1983, 1984, 1985, 1986, 1987 by Playboy.

Every effort has been made to trace the ownership or source of all illustrated material for the purpose of giving proper credit. We regret any inadvertent error concerning the attribution given to any such materials and will be pleased to make the appropriate acknowledgments in any future printings.

Visit DC Comics online at www.dccomics.com or on America Online at keyword: DCComics.

GRATEFUL THANKS AND A TIP OF THE WOOZY WINKS CHAPEAU TO:

- Dick Cole for his generosity in so freely sharing family memories as well as memorabilia.

- Creig & Marie Flessel and Gil Fox, whose lucid and loving recollections conjured up a touchingly real Jack Cole.

- Ron Goulart, Jerry DeFuccio, R.C. Harvey, Rob Stolzer, and Gil Kane's ectoplasm. Their scholarship and files were invaluable in navigating this terrain. (Now, now Ron—no cracks about placing dollar amounts on the value please!)

- Paul Karasik, whose collection and intelligent enthusiasm grace so many of these pages.

- Michelle Urry, whose friendship (and Playboy club keys) opened the doors to Cole's later incarnations.

- Hugh Hefner, for his articulate and acute insights into Cole and his work.

- David Remnick and Ann Goldstein of *The New Yorker* for their support and editing of this text as it first appeared in those august pages . . . and to Steve Korté of DC for helping it morph into its current form.

- Francoise (always!)

a.s.

- Steve Korté (yes, I know this is a double—but that's a major theme later, you'll see), dear friend and editor, without whom this book would never have come together.

- Jules Feiffer, for writing *The Great Comic Book Heroes*, and introducing me to Plastic Man for the first time.

- Chin-Yee Lai, for her invaluable help in putting it together.

- J. D. McClatchy, who didn't divorce me when I told him I was doing this book.

O N E

Disguised as a red, black, and yellow throw rug, our hero cocks one ear up to listen in on two hoods huddled at the table that rests on him. In the next panel he literally hangs out at an art museum, above a label that reads "Abstract," his body now distorted into a red, black, and yellow bebop-cubist composition in order to eavesdrop on two cheap gunsels out gallery-hopping. And in the panel after that, two molls gossip from tenement windows across an alley while our protean hero continues his stakeout camouflaged as a red, black, and yellow line of laundry flapping between them.

This manic spritz of images appeared in a 1950 issue of *Plastic Man*, one of the last written and drawn by Jack Cole, a tragically short-lived comic book giant. *Plastic Man*, like most of Cole's achievements, can be found mainly in those plastic bags collectors use to stash their rare slow-burning forest fires of newsprint. Although I'm slightly embarrassed to confess to being in love with a super-hero comic, Jack Cole's *Plastic Man* belongs high on any adult's How to Avoid Prozac list, up there with the best of S. J. Perelman, Laurel and Hardy, Damon Runyon, Tex Avery, and the Marx Brothers.

Above and right: *Plastic Man* #25 (September 1950)

Cole's comics have helped me feel reconciled to the misleading word "comic," which often keeps my medium of choice from getting any respect.

Many otherwise literate people, even those who have long since crossed the high-low divide and welcomed comic strips like *Krazy Kat* and *Little Nemo* into the canon of twentieth-century cultural achievement—right up there next to Picasso's paintings and Joyce's novels—remain predisposed against comic *books*. Of course most comic books really *are* junk, just like our parents said, but so is most painting and fiction. The lowly comic book has a lot of strikes against it, not least a residual public distaste left over from Senator Estes Kefauver's 1950s crime hearings on juvenile delinquency, which scapegoated the whole medium as a species of pornography for tots. The hearings forced a draconian "self-regulating" Comics Code Authority on the publishers; the edict stamped out the reckless excesses of the crime, war, and horror comics (categories that tended to appeal to an older audience of G.I.s and other adults), and left lobotomized super heroes and innocuous funny animals as virtually the only survivors on the newsstands. We've often committed some of our most censorious follies in the guise of protecting our children.

It's a tribute to the medium's appeal that the comic book has bounced back from the grave several times in its history, although the industry has never been as close to death as now. Near suicidal publishing and marketing decisions—for example, aiming at a narrow collectors' market rather than reaching out to mainstream audiences—have left the industry in a depressed state. Television almost killed what remained of comics in the mid-fifties; now new computer-generated special-effects technologies have robbed comics of even their near monopoly on primal visual fantasy. Comic books must reposition themselves—possibly as Art—in order to survive as anything more than part of a feeder system for Hollywood. Otherwise, like vaudeville, they will vanish.

Art? It now seems natural to see Orson Welles's *Touch of Evil* or a Howard Hawks western at New York's Museum of Modern Art, but a generation of aestheticians like Manny Farber had to show people how to see movies for such events to become plausible. In a landmark 1962 essay in *Film Culture*, Farber looked at B movies with a painter's eyes and championed the neglected genre films he loved. He contrasted "the idea of art as an expensive hunk of well-regulated area . . . shrieking with preciosity, fame, ambition," with art made "where the spotlight of culture is nowhere in evidence, so that the craftsman can be ornery, wasteful, stubbornly self-involved, doing go-for-broke art and not caring what comes of it." This he called a "termite-tapeworm-fungus-moss art . . . that goes always forward, eating its own boundaries, and likely as not leaves nothing in its path other than signs of eager, industrious unkempt activity." The comic book form has always swarmed with termites, never more so than in the Golden Age, which collectors date from the spring of 1938, when Superman first turned the ephemeral periodicals into a major fad, until the devastation brought by the Comics Code in late 1954. It was a time when comics always traveled below critical radar and offered a direct gateway into the unrestrained dream life of their creators—lurid, violent, funny, and sometimes sublime.

Plas bursts out of 2-D space on the cover of *Police Comics* #38 (January 1945).

TWO

Jack Cole, whose comic book career started a year before that Golden Age and ended precisely with it, was born in December 1914, in the small coal-mining and industrial town of New Castle, in western Pennsylvania. His father, a Methodist Sunday-school teacher for twenty years, owned a dry-goods store and was a popular local performer, playing the bones in King Cole's Corn Crackers; his mother had been a grade-school teacher. Jack, the third of six children, was introspective, imaginative, high-spirited, and graced with a pronounced sense of humor. A childhood passion for newspaper strips like Elzie Segar's *Thimble Theater* (featuring Popeye), George McManus's *Bringing Up Father,* and Rube Goldberg's *Boob McNutt* blossomed into a lifelong desire to draw a syndicated strip of his own. His formal art training, beyond copying his favorites to crack their physiognomic code, consisted of mail-order lessons from the Landon School of Cartooning. When he was fifteen, Cole secretly saved up his school lunch money to pay for the course, smuggling sandwiches from home in the hollowed-out pages of a book. Two years later he again proved his strength of character by bicycling alone to Los Angeles and back, a seven-thousand-mile adventure he later recounted in his first sale, an illustrated feature for *Boys' Life.*

After graduating from high school, Cole eloped with his childhood sweetheart, Dorothy Mahoney. Drawing cartoons at night and working at the local American Can Factory by day, he remained in his parents' home until his mother found out about the secret marriage and suggested that he live with his wife. Dick Cole, his youngest brother, still remembers the Pop-Art-before-its-time furniture Jack playfully improvised out of printed tin sheets brought home from his job. American Can, however, clearly didn't offer him the creative outlet he was searching for, and in 1936, at the age of twenty-two, he quit. Borrowing five hundred dollars from family friends and local merchants (such as the supportive druggist who posted Cole's cartoons in his store), he moved to Greenwich Village with Dorothy to seek his fortune as a cartoonist. In a dutiful letter that he sent home after settling in, he put a positive spin on his career prospects, praising Dorothy's steadfastness, and reassuring his parents that he hadn't been corrupted by the big city:

*Every kid wants to grow up to be as good
as his parents, and I, being no exception
have about as high a goal as could be
possible to strive for. Have tried to do*

Cole in his home studio (1938)

A Boy and His Bike

By Jack Ralph Cole

Illustrations by the Author

I WAS spring; the calendar read a quarter past 1932. Grass grew green. Birds warbled as they watched our old maple tree slowly unclench her fist-like buds into countless emerald leaves. And along with this resurrection of vegetation there came to me an irresistible desire to go somewhere—anywhere.

I had hoped to see the Olympic Games being held that summer at Los Angeles, California. In fact, Dick—likewise suffering from wanderlust—and myself were already rounding out plans for making the journey via "Model T"; then Dick's family moved from town. I could not afford to buy and operate an automobile alone, so I had to find a cheaper mode of transportation.

"Can I hitchhike out, dad?" I asked.

His answer was emphatically no.

Finally, as a last hope, I sought permission to go by bicycle, and, *mirabile dictu*, the necessary permission was granted.

By July 11, all was in readiness: bicycle overhauled, route mapped out, equipment gathered, clothing packed. The following morning, at dawn, my journey began, and, glancing back over my shoulder, I said good-by to the old homestead, to New Castle, and, later in the day, to Pennsylvania itself. Like all greenhorns, I was sure that the more the equipment, the better the trip. In addition to the clothing I wore, my outfit consisted of: two blankets, a pup tent, raincoat, three pairs of socks, underclothing, bathing suit, sweater, bicycle tools, medicine kit, sewing kit, canteen, cooking utensils, food, Bible, flashlight, paper, pencils, towels, soap, and a mouth organ.

Jack Cole, and the bicycle which replaced Bessy

Fourteen hours of continuous pedaling, that first day, caused severe cramps in both legs. This was my first time on a bike in two years. I crawled off and set up camp beside a cemetery. Then, after preparing a rather slipshod meal, I fell into undisturbed sleep. The first hundred miles proved to be by far the most trying. Each succeeding day became less and less tedious, and correspondingly more enjoyable.

. . . I came upon a granddaddy rattlesnake

Near Indianapolis, Bessy, my trusty steed, began to wheeze and buckle slightly at the knees, protesting such an excess in baggage, so I gathered all unnecessary articles, including the raincoat, and shipped them home C. O. D.

Up at daybreak each morning, I would cook breakfast, pack up, and set out, stopping only for an occasional snack, or perhaps to fill my radiator at some wayside pump. I was often able to buy from a farmer a quart of milk for two cents, or half a dozen eggs for a nickel. Thus living was inexpensive. My greatest extravagance was a quart of ice cream a day. Old Sol sang daily to the tune of ninety degrees in the shade. To find camping sites was no problem; fields were plentiful, or sometimes a considerate farmer would permit the use of his hayloft. The most preferable spot, though, was to be found near tourist camps, where I stood the chance of getting a refreshing shower bath if the proprietor happened to be in a congenial mood.

One week on the road took me to Saint Louis, Missouri. Two days later, while stopping for the

find my face a mass of stinging, swelling welts. Mosquitoes—hundreds of them—were attacking me savagely from every angle, and I was forced to spend the remainder of the night with a wet towel over my face, leaving only my nose protruding.

Mother and dad had promised to write often, so the first thing I did, upon reaching Kansas City the next day, was to make a bee line for the post office—which was closed. This meant an overnight stay. A fifty-cent hotel furnished sleeping accommodations. Here I received the first glimpse of myself in a mirror since starting. I could hardly recognize myself! The mirror reflected a six-foot lad whose 150 pounds had diminished to 135 pounds in ten days (this explained the sudden slack in his trousers). His face was swollen abnormally—one eye completely closed—from mosquito bites; broiling sun had chipped off most of the top soil from his nose, leaving it a brilliant crimson hue; his head, which a friend had graciously shaved just before the trip, was sunburned to the peeling point.

I had left a loaf of bread on the bicycle that night, wrapped in my swimming suit (you'd be surprised how a damp suit maintains the freshness in bread), and in the morning, when I went to get it, I discovered that rats had completely demolished both bread and water togs. But rivers were becoming scarce, so the loss was not tragic.

KANSAS plains offer a veritable paradise for cyclists. With an assisting breeze, it was not at all impossible to cover 150 miles a day. Dodge City, Kansas, proved to be—to me at least—the doorway to the romantic West. Here I saw with wonder my first cactus plant, rattlesnake, horned toad, and prairie dog. But soon these sights became commonplace.

Although most of the roads were in good condition, there were some whose construction plainly vetoed bicycle traveling, those of gravel or sand. Pedaling through sand is like tramping through deep snow *sans* snowshoes.

About Dessy, she was the height of inconsideration and indiscretion. While descending a precipitous mountain pass in Colorado, I naturally applied the brakes. Instantly everything collapsed. The repair job that followed bit so mercilessly into my pocketbook that a request for currency was promptly rushed eastward.

On this same day, near sundown, I was idling along at a leisurely pace, when all at once a loud report sounded, and simultaneously a bullet whistled directly over my head. About one hundred feet away stood an intoxicated Mexican, gun in hand, evidently enjoying the time of his life, but my sense of humor was not keen enough to appreciate such a joke. Bessy certainly could cover ground with the proper incentive—those succeeding twenty miles passed in a blur.

Nights in New Mexico's highlands are filled with enchantment. The bright moon shines down upon white mountain peaks; the air is cool and refreshing. Occasionally a distant coyote interrupts

Westward ho!

balance the beauty, though, were steep and snake-like roads, opposing my efforts of shin with all the forces of gravity. Travel was consequently slowed down.

Flat tires? By the good grace of Lady Luck, only once did this happen. Four miles west of Flagstaff, Arizona, a sharp piece of gravel accomplished the deed. Instead of back tracking four miles, I plunged on ahead, hoping to buy a new tire at the next town. To my chagrin, I straggled 150 miles—walking fifty and receiving a lift for the remainder—to Kingman, Arizona, before finally locating a place where tires were sold.

Between Kingman and Los Angeles lie 250 miles of continuous desert, and the next day, when I reached Needles, California, situated in the very heart of it all, the temperature registered 120 degrees in the shade. After dining on ice cream I rode out into the sweltering heat. Ten miles up-grade I pumped. Not a house, tree, nor even a signboard. My head began to reel and it seemed difficult to breathe, so, pouring the entire contents of my canteen over my body, I turned about and scurried back to Needles. I started out again after dark.

All through that night and the following day I rode, and reached Los Angeles about sundown. Forty hours without sleep! I went to bed at once.

The 3000-mile journey had been covered in days, averaging from 100 to 150 miles a day. Bessy was so utterly fatigued from such an ordeal, that, like the "one hoss shay," she simply went to pieces. There was nothing to do but abandon her, old friends though we had been.

No story is complete without a certain degree of pathos. The sad part of my story is that, after coming this far for the express purpose of seeing the Olympics, I did not have enough money to gain admittance. I remained in Los Angeles a week in a cheap hotel.

When my clothes from home arrived, I hiked to Long Beach, and spent a most enjoyable week at the home of friends. Early one morning we drove up into the San Bernardino mountains, to try our luck at gold mining, and we did manage to pan out about twenty-five cents worth of the metal.

I had relatives living near San Francisco, so I decided to pay them a visit next. To be suddenly catapulted from the role of poor vagabond to fêted guest is bewildering. Tennis, theaters, motor trips, operas, swimming, boat rides, field club—all wedged tightly into

I could hardly recognize myself

two weeks, left me nearly breathless.

In spite of the hospitality showered upon me, I began now to want to go home. When I disclosed my intention of hitchhiking the distance, my uncle thrust two ominous thumbs downward, and offered—or rather insisted upon—a bus ride home at his expense. When an irresistible force meets an

---

Cole's first professional sale, to *Boys' Life* in 1935, recounts his 1932 adventure bicycling all across America and back.

things as you would do them, but unfortunately I am ruled by my heart rather than my head, and sometimes slip up (or rather, many times). I have never told you this before, but in case you are interested, I have never taken a drink of beer or liquer yet and never mean to—don't smoke—cuss some but have never used His name in a vain expression.

Though he eventually smoked, drank moderately, and possibly even took God's name in vain, Cole was always conscientious. In time he even paid his debts to the New Castle folk who sponsored him, but after a year of trying to break into magazines and newspapers he had whittled his stake down to five cents. According to comics historian Ron Goulart, author of the invaluable *Focus on Jack Cole* published by Fantagraphics in 1986, Cole found himself working for about twenty dollars a week in a factory again: at Harry "A" Chesler's comic book "sweat-

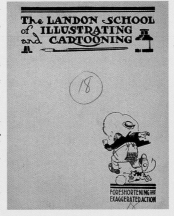

shop" at Fifth Avenue and Twenty-ninth Street, set up to provide new content for publishers unable to find any newspaper strips worth reprinting. The first ten-cent comic book, *Famous Funnies,* published in 1934, consisted of reduced-scale color reprints of *Mutt and Jeff, The Bungle Family,* and other popular syndicated features; green kid cartoonists worked elbow to elbow with old pulp illustrators, down-on-their-luck painters, and other has-beens and never-wases to pioneer a new art form at cut rates that could compete with the low-priced syndicate retreads.

Marshall McLuhan has written that every new medium cannibalizes the content of the medium that preceded it (the movies, for example, were once called "photoplays"), and the comic book bears this idea out: pale imitations of *Dick Tracy* and *Mandrake the Magician* were the anemic norm until 1938, when the first issue of *Action Comics* presented a caped Übermensch from the planet Krypton who fought for Truth, Justice, and the American Way—a crackbrained idea by two Jewish kids from Cleveland that really made the new medium fly. *Action!* The title nails the basic appeal of the new four-color pulps: Crimson Avengers, Purple Zombies, Green Masks, Blue Beetles, Blue Bolts, Blue Streaks, White Streaks, and Silver Streaks started zipping through the sky, hitting the newsstands and one another.

Young Jack Cole learns about foreshortening in these corrected sketches for the Landon School.

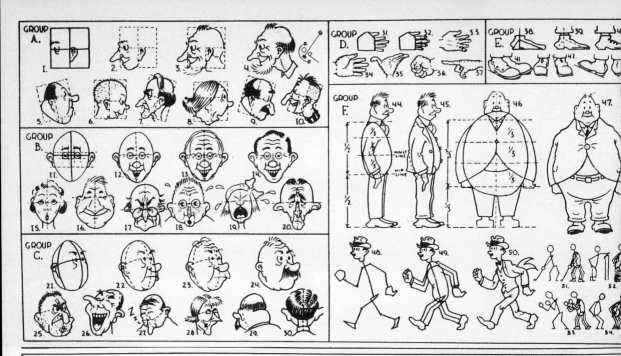

Have you a desire to cartoon? Then you can cartoon! Let me stamp this indelibly upon your minds. YOU CAN CARTOON! It is immaterial whether or not you are endowed with natural artistic ability; if you but possess the will and determination you can learn to draw just as you have learned to write. Every cartoonist in the country has had nothing more to begin with than you or I—merely a desire. I cannot guarantee to make you a success as a cartoonist—no one can do that—but I can tell you how you may make yourself one.

The beginner's equipment need not be extravagant: a ruler, eraser, black India ink, pen, pencil, brush, and a few pen points constitute the only necessary articles. (I use a Gillott's No. 1158 or a Hunt No. 153 pen point mostly. But what suits one may displease another, so try out several different types and select the ones you like best). A drawing board and "T" square are also desirable. Any paper with a hard, smooth surface will do for ink work.

Let us first take up the construction of the head. Ability to caricature is the ability to recognize outstanding physical features of the face, and then to emphasize these features by exaggeration. To draw a side view, the easiest process is to construct a square, bisecting it with horizontal and vertical lines. No. 1 on the accompanying chart illustrates this step. Position of the eye is always as shown in No. 1, on the horizontal guide line. Place the ear at the intersection of the two guidelines. Approximately halfway between eyebrow and point of chin (No. 2), the nose terminates. Now draw the mouth and chin, placing the mouth about one-third the distance from nose to chin. Complete the outline of the head (No. 3) and block in hair. After you have finished the sketch, apply pen lines and erase pencil

lines (No. 4).

Variations of this rule are quite numerous, however. If the subject is to be a fat person, place the horizontal guideline slightly below (No. 6) the center of the square. A child should have a very prominent forehead to counterbalance its receding chin. Use a rectangle instead of a square (No. 7) when drawing thin persons.

Due to bisymmetrical structure, front view drawings are more difficult than side view drawings. No. 11 shows an oval drawn to represent the intended shape of the head. Like the square, it is bisected vertically and horizontally. Place eyes on the horizontal line, about the width of one eye apart. Care should be exercised not to get one eye larger than or below the level of the other. Mistakes of this sort tend to brand a cartoon as amateurish. The same applies to the size and location of the ears. Guide lines are used as shown in No. 11, to obtain even proportion in eyes and ears. Nose, mouth, and chin are drawn next (No. 12), then the hair is outlined (No. 13). No. 14 shows the completed head. Compare Nos. 15 through 20, for relative position of eyes and shape of heads.

Most widely used in cartooning is the "angle" view—a combination front and side view. No. 21 shows how guide lines are arranged to aid placement of features. Follow steps 22, 23, and 24 closely in working out your own drawings. Remember that only one ear is visible in most angle views. This is also true in angle views from the rear (No. 29). In drawing a direct rear view, avoid a "doorknob" effect by extending the neck lines clear to the base of the hair, instead of chopping them off at the bottom of the head (No. 30).

For practice work, draw a group of funny noses, mouths, whiskers and hair; then draw faces, using a different combination of features each time. Draw,

draw, draw!

Without expression, a cartoon lacks the punch to put it over. Notice the different expressions in groups B and C; memorize the various lines that govern them. An excellent idea is to clip from old magazines and newspapers as many different types of faces and expressions as possible. Keep these in a scrapbook, with name of expression and type of face written under each. Study them; use them as a guide to making up your own cartoons.

Another ideal way of learning expressions is to make faces in the mirror. I used to stand in front of my dresser for hours, laughing, pouting, frowning, sighing, etc. all the while recording on paper the characteristic wrinkles.

Group D demonstrates the structure of hands. Pay strict attention to the relative length of fingers and placement of thumb. Look at your own hands—draw them in different positions. Always employ the five pointed object (No. 31) in drawing hands.

Logically following hands are feet. The use of a triangle, such as the one pictured in No. 38, greatly facilitates in the learning of the correct shape of the foot. You may encounter some difficulties with hands and feet, but constant practice will eliminate these.

After you have mastered the head, hands, and feet, learn to draw comic bodies. No. 44 gives the proportions of a comic figure in side position. Now, in actual anatomy, the head is a fraction less than one-seventh of the entire body, but in a cartoon, the ratio is reduced to one fifth or one sixth, depending upon the type of figure to be drawn. Observe that the legs of a normal man (No. 44) are as long as the torso.

Never start the sleeve of a coat at the neck; begin it about one-third down the body, as No. 44 shows. Locate elbows

and knees at the middle of arms and le respectively.

For figures in action, the skelet method eliminates a lot of guesswork. you follow the process described in N 48, 49, and 50, it won't be long before y can draw a comic body in many positio Memorize the various wrinkles in t clothing of figures in group F. Nos. through 54 show how to draw skeletons action, and how to form the body arou them.

That is the surest—and the easies way to draw human figures.

ODDS AND ENDS

1. Leave plenty of border around dra ings—at least an inch at both sides top, and two inches at the bottom.

2. Carelessness has no place in makeup of a cartoonist. I sometimes sp 0 to 10 hours on one drawing befor am satisfied.

3. Draw mostly about subjects fami to you.

4. Ideas to be illustrated should ne offend races, religions or persons (espec ly those with physical afflictions).

5. Bear in mind that most reproducti of cartoons in magazines and newspap are about one fourth their normal size, draw your pen lines twice as thick as normally do.

6. Keep your old drawings for c parison with later ones, so that you tell how much progress has been made

7. Get plenty of action into cartoon

8. Be original in everything you d never copy.

9. Practice making pen lines until can draw without the slightest jerki in your pilot hand.

10. Get your work published so where, if possible, as reproduction enable you to find your weak points n readily.

Remember YOU CAN CARTOON!

Smash Comics #72 (August 1947)

Smash Comics #34 (July 194

Cole thrived, first in the Chesler shop and then as a freelancer, working against tight deadlines and learning in print how to take advantage of the flexible panel layouts and dynamic pages that these books demanded. He was an "all-around man," writing as well as drawing, even lettering and sometimes coloring his own material. He started out doing screwball filler pages and then graduated to the longer and more lucrative "straight" stuff, though even his most illustrative work happily betrayed his roots in loopy-doodle cartooning. His early straight work was crazily bent: Mantoka (a supernaturally empowered Native American medicine man who takes revenge on evil Caucasians), The Comet (whose disintegrating rays shoot out of his eyes whenever he crosses them to melt down bad guys), and, for *Silver Streak Comics,* The Claw (the ultimate Yellow Peril, a fanged Asian warlord who can get taller than King Kong when aroused) all displayed a feverish imagination, verve, and a cheerful streak of perverse violence.

By the end of 1940, Cole had begun work-

ing for Quality Comics, Everett ("Busy") Arnold's newly launched line of publications. Quality became home base for the rest of Cole's comic book career. The feel and look of the Quality Comics house style had been established by Will Eisner, creator of *The Spirit,* whose work was to have a major influence on Cole. Eisner, who is now in his eighties and still doing significant comics, had studied painting and hoped to become a theatrical set designer; he was more culturally sophisticated than Cole, who had been shaped mainly by pulps, movies, comic strips, and the other early comic books—which were mostly influenced by more of the same. Cole's first sustained work for Quality was *Midnight,* a feature intended by the pragmatic Arnold as a clone of *The Spirit*—just in case Eisner, who was in the unique position of owning his own character, were to be drafted and die or otherwise leave Quality. Cole learned important lessons in narrative and structural coherence from this apprenticeship, and brought his singular sense of humor and fantasy to the project.

Midnight began inauspiciously enough (in *Smash Comics* #18, January 1941) as an in-house plagiarism of Will Eisner's *Spirit*. Within a y Cole's exuberance, oddness, and rapidly maturing style built *Midnight* into *Smash Comics*'s cover star until the title folded in 1949. Parody or commenting on The Spirit's minstrel sidekick, Ebony White, Cole introduced Gabby, a talking monkey, as Midnight's constant companio

A few months after *Midnight* came *Plastic Man*, starting as a minor feature in *Police Comics*, but soon to become the star of that anthology. Inspired by sideshow freaks, Cole planned to call the character the India Rubber Man. Arnold astutely suggested that it might be bouncier to name him after the miracle substance that was reshaping the modern world. In 1943, when Plastic Man expanded into his own book, Cole explained the morphing hero to new readers: "If you should see a man standing on the street and reaching into the top window of a sky-scraper . . . that's not astigmatism—it's Plastic Man! . . . If you happen upon a gent all bent up like a pretzel . . . don't dunk him . . . it's Plastic Man! All this and bouncing too, you'll see when the rubber man and his pal Woozy Winks gamble their lives in—The Game of Death."

Left: Cover by Cole for *Silver Streak Comics* #6 (September 1940)
Below: Back cover to *Silver Streak Comics* #5 (July 1940)

the end of
939, Cole began
iting *Silver
treak Comics* for
at became Lev
eason's Comic
ouse, inventing
e Claw (an
iental demon
o made
ng the
erciless look
e Mother
resa). In
sue 6—hot
the heels of
nely Comics'
ulti-issue
ttles between
e Human
rch and The
b-Mariner—
e initiated
)aredevil vs.
e Claw," a
mented
ossover epic
at helped
fine the Golden
e of comics.

THE CLAW RETURNS!

Appearing as a secondary feature in the first issue of *Police Comics* (August 1941), Plas grew to become leading man by the fifth issue. Cole's already considerable skills as an artist and story-teller grew startlingly as well. The first Plastic Man stories veered between melodrama and Grand Guignol; increasingly, they were laced with comedy.

In 1943 Cole allowed himself to stretch toward sentimentality and may have even achieved pathos. "The Eyes Have It" (here reprinted from *Police Comics* #22) is an over-the-top tale of child abuse (possibly informed by Cole's own inability to have kids). Ambitiously, the story reaches for the laughs, tears, and shudders trumpeted on its cover blurb.

The "Burp the Twerp" series of short fillers by Cole (using the pen name Ralph Johns, based on his first and middle names) was idiosyncratic even by his standards. The one that follows is from *Police Comics* #29 (April 1944).

Above: *Plastic Man #22, March 1950*

PLASTIC MAN OF THE F.B.I. ... AND HIS FRIEND, WOOZY WINKS, ARE OUT STROLLING, ONE FINE EVENING . . . .

LOOK AT THAT MOON, WOOZ!

ROMANTIC, AIN'T IT? ... I CAN JUST SEE MYSELF AND JANE RUSSELL HOLDING HANDS IN THE PARK!...

...WE SIGH... WE CUDDLE... THEN SHE LIFTS HER LIPS TO MINE... AND...

THUMP THUMP

SMACK!

C'MERE YOU!

WOW! CAN THAT GAL KISS!!

WHY, THAT INHUMAN RAT!! LOOK!

HE'S DUNKING THAT KID IN WATER!

RUN AWAY FROM THE SPHINX, WILL YOU?

GLUB BLUB

GA

UG.

YOU KNOW BETTER THAN TO TREAT A CHILD LIKE THAT!

POOR TYKE'S HALF DROWNED!

GAS

GAS

DON'T CRY SON! ... WE WON'T LET HIM HURT YOU!

WHAT'S YOUR NAME? WHY'S HE TRYIN' TO HURT YOU?

WHY...WHY... HE CAN'T TALK! HE'S TRYING TO TELL US SOMETHING, BUT THE WORDS WON'T COME OUT!

LOOK AT THOSE EYES! THEY REFLECT TERROR! LET'S TURN THIS LUG OVER TO THE CITY POLICE!

HOP ON, HOOLEY!

GUN IT, GUYS! THAT'S PLASTIC MAN!

WE KNOW IT!

OH-OH! TOO LATE! HE ESCAPED!

SSSS SSS

TAT-TAT TAT-TAT-TAT

WOW!.. THE WAY THINGS ARE DEVELOPING, MAYBE EVEN YOUR F.B.I. WOULD BE INT'RESTED IN THIS CASE!

COULD BE!... I'LL SEE WHAT CHIEF BRANNER SAYS ABOUT IT... COME ON!

BAM!

AW, CHIEF! HAVE A HEART!... I'LL HANDLE THE CASE MYSELF!!

IT'S HARD TO RESIST SUCH A PLEADING PAIR OF BLUE EYES.......BUT...

THERE IS NO ROOM FOR SENTIMENTALITY IN THE F.B.I.!! THIS CASE IS CLEARLY OUT OF OUR JURISDICTION... IT BELONGS TO THE LOCAL POLICE!

NOW GET THE LITTLE RASCAL OUT OF HERE BEFORE I FALL PREY TO HIS HYPNOTIC GAZE AND WEAKEN, MYSELF!

CHIEF!... HE'S GONE!!

...IF THIS IS ONE OF YOUR... HE IS GONE!

KIDNAPPED! RIGHT UNDER MY NOSE!

GONE! ...THAT PUTS THE CASE RIGHT IN OUR LAP, AFTER ALL!

?

BUT AT THAT MOMENT...

PLASTIC MAN!

WAS THAT YOU WHO CALLED HEADQUARTERS AND HOLLERED FOR HELP?

NO, BUT I LOVE WHOEVER IT WAS!

AIR!

WE TRACED THE CALL!

THERE'S A BOAT BASE BELOW... WE MAY BE ABLE TO NAB THE THUGS BEFORE THEY ESCAPE!

??
ACK!
?
?

WHOA, THERE, SPHINX!! A WORD WITH YOU!!

BEFORE YOU SAY ANYTHING, GENTS, I MUST TELL YOU THAT THE BOAT HAS LEFT AND YOU ARE GOING TO LET ME GO SCOT FREE!

SEZ WHO?

PRETTY CONFIDENT, AREN'T YOU?

YOU SEE, IF MY MEN DON'T HEAR FROM ME IN TWO HOURS, THEY HAVE ORDERS TO DROWN THE KIDS!...

GOOD EVENING, SUCKERS!

CAN YOU BEAT THAT? -- WALKED OUT FREE AS A BEE!

AND WE CAN'T STOP HIM!

HE'S A SLICK ONE, ALL RIGHT!

I FEEL HELPLESS AS A JELLY FISH!

LATER, ANCHORED OFF SHORE, IS ---- LOOK CLOSELY, NOW ---- A LOW-LYING BOAT, CAMOUFLAGED TO LOOK LIKE THE SURROUNDING WATER!

AND WITHIN THE BOAT...

IT'S SPHINX! ... HE SAYS TO DUMP THE BRATS! THE HEAT'S ON!

WELL ... LET'S GET IT OVER WITH, THEN!

I HATE TO DO THIS... BUT ORDERS IS ----- WHAT ARE YOU STARING AT?

STOP IT!! DO YOU HEAR?

WHAT'S THE USE? I--I CAN'T DO IT! ... THOSE EYES! THERE'S SOMETHING ABOUT THEM THAT GET ME!

YOU'RE NUTS!

GIMME TH' GAT, SOFTIE!... I'LL SHOW YOU HOW!

NO, SPIKE! I WON'T LET YOU!

I SAID GIMME THAT OHHHHHH!

SPIKE! SPIKE!... WHAT HAVE I DONE? ... I DIDN'T MEAN IT HONEST!!

BAM

DIRTY SWINE! IF I DIE... SO... DO... YOU!

NO... YOU'RE BITING MY JUGULAR VEIN NO! NO! NO!

OUTSIDE, LIGHTNING FLASHES, MARKING THE END OF ONE STORM AND THE BEGINNING OF ANOTHER!...

HIGHER AND HIGHER THE SEA RAGES OVER THE DEAD MEN AND THIRTY HELPLESS CHILDREN!...

BUT INSIDE, BRIGHT EYES IS MOVED TO FEVERISH ACTION...

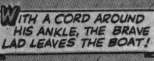

WITH A CORD AROUND HIS ANKLE, THE BRAVE LAD LEAVES THE BOAT!

AND FINALLY, EXHAUSTED, SINKS BENEATH THE ANGRY WAVES!!

HE STRUGGLES VAINLY AGAINST THE STORM!

AND SEVERAL MILES AWAY IN A HIDDEN SHACK...

WELL...THAT'S THAT! HEH-HEH...WE CAN GET ANOTHER SUPPLY AND START UP AGAIN WHEN THE HEAT'S OFF!

SO YOU WENT BACK ON YOUR WORD, EH?.. ORDERED THE KIDS KILLED EVEN AFTER WE LET YOU GO!!

COUNTERMAND THAT ORDER, SPHINX!

YOU!!

I'D GLADLY DO IT...ONLY... HA-HA!...THE RADIO'S OUT OF ORDER!

RIP!

OF ALL THE---

I'VE BEEN WAITING TO KILL BRIGHT EYES FOR A LONG TIME...AND YOU CAN'T DO A THING ABOUT IT!!

WHY DO YOU HATE HIM SO?

WHY... IT'S A **BOAT!** ... A PERFECT JOB OF CAMOUFLAGING!...

BACK ON SHORE...

KID... KID... *PUFF* YOU JUST **GOTTA** COME OUT OF IT! *PUFF–PUFF* *PUFF*

PLEASE LET HIM LIVE ... I KNOW I'VE NO RIGHT TO ASK FAVORS " BUT HE'S SO YOUNG... ...CAN'T YOU... PLEASE? " FOR HIS SAKE...

HE ... HE... **MOVED!**... ...HE'S **ALIVE!**...

SNIFF OH, THANK YOU, **THANK** YOU, **THANK** YOU!

WHY ARE YOU CRYING, SIR?

YOU'RE **TALKING,** TOO! ... BUT I THOUGHT—

EVIDENTLY THE SHOCK BROUGHT MY VOICE BACK!

BUT WHAT CAUSED YOU TO **LOSE** YOUR VOICE?... SPHINX?

WELL ... YOU SEE, SIR... IT'S A LONG STORY! AS YOU SEE BY THIS PICTURE, I HAD A SWEET MOTHER, BUT A CRUEL FATHER!... ONE NIGHT LAST YEAR .....

...FATHER, IN A FIT OF RAGE, KILLED POOR MOTHER! ... I WAS STUNNED ... SPEECHLESS...

DADDY! DON'T! NO!!

...IN FACT, SO SHOCKED WAS I, THAT I LOST MY POWER OF SPEECH!...

ONE WORD OUT OF YOU ABOUT THIS AND IT'LL BE YOUR **LAST!**

NOT KNOWING I HAD LOST MY VOICE, HE MOVED TO A DESOLATE OLD SHACK, AFRAID I WOULD EXPOSE HIS DEED...

HE KEPT ME LOCKED AND CHAINED FOR WEEKS ON END... HE THOUGHT I WAS SIMPLY REFUSING TO TALK...

I DON'T KNOW WHY... BUT HE COULDN'T STAND MY GAZE... MAYBE I MADE HIM FEEL GUILTY... HE LOVED TO TORTURE ME...

HERE... MAYBE *THIS'LL* LOOSEN YOUR TONGUE!

ONE NIGHT SOME INQUISITIVE NEIGHBORS SAW HIM BEATING ME....

BOYS... ARE WE GOIN' TO STAND FER THIS?

LIKE *HECK* WE ARE!

SO THEY DRAGGED HIM OUT, TARRED AND FEATHERED HIM....

OHHWWHHHH

AND LEFT HIM IN A SWAMP TO DIE.....

IT SEEMS MY EYES DO THINGS TO PEOPLE... ANYWAY, I WAS ADOPTED BY A MR. AND MRS. GRIMLEY....

JUST THINK, DEAR... *OUR SON!*

HE'S JUST WHAT WE'VE BEEN NEEDING!

I WAS WHAT THEY NEEDED, ALL RIGHT... FOR A *BLIND ACT*... MR. GRIMLEY SAID I MOVED PEOPLE TO GIVE....

HMMM.... THAT KID WOULD BE AN ASSET IN MY BUSINESS!

WHEN THE *SPHINX* SAW THE GRIP I HAD ON FOLKS, HE OFFERED TO BUY ME FROM THE GRIMLEYS....

SELL OUR BOY?... WE COULDN'T THINK OF IT!

HOW MUCH WILL YOU GIVE US?

THREE

Plastic Man wore a V-necked red rubber leotard accessorized by a wide black-and-yellow-striped belt and very cool tinted goggles. He started life as Eel O'Brian, a low-life gangster accidentally doused by some unnamed acid while committing a robbery. He was saved by a reclusive order of monks who recognized that his villainy was the result of an unhappy childhood. They nursed him back to health and in a memorable couple of panels he discovered his gift:

and soon forgot about being Eel O'Brian.

It says something about Cole's superego, if not his super hero, that he often cast reformed villains as his principals. Woozy Winks, Plastic Man's Robin, was hardly a Boy Wonder. He entered the series as a miscreant, the Man Who Cannot Be Harmed, having chosen a life of crime on the basis of a coin-toss. Several issues later his powers diminished so that he became the Man Whom Nature Protects (Sometimes),

Police Comics #1 (August 1941)

The acid bath had given him the ability to violate the laws of physics; the monks gave him the will to defend the laws of men, first as part of the police force, then later as a special agent for the FBI. His FBI chief, sporting one of the most peculiar comb-overs in comics, was the authority figure in Plastic Man's tiny nuclear family. Nobody knew that Plastic Man and the gangster Eel O'Brian were the same person. His secret identity—as a public enemy he himself was supposed to capture—was too limiting a concept for a hero who could be literally anything he wanted to be. Superman and the tribe that grew from that template have a mere two identities: they're binary. Plas, as his friends called him, was multiphrenic and illimitable,

and he eventually settled in as an all too mortal bungler, a skirt-chaser, and an occasional pickpocket. He was a slovenly, scrotum-cheeked rube in a straw hat and green polka-dot shirt who looked a bit like Alfred Hitchcock. Providing a meatball-shaped counterweight to Plastic Man's spaghetti, his direct forebear was Popeye's pal Wimpy—another absurdly self-centered glutton with an equally unwarranted high self-regard. In a more "straight" comic book reality, Woozy would have provided comic relief.

Naturally enough, Cole resembled both his leads: like Woozy, he was soft bodied, somewhat disheveled, and no city slicker; like Plastic Man, he was tall, pointy nosed, and "very likable . . .

Cole's first strip for Quality was this two-page "Wun Cloo" filler in *Smash Comics* #17 (December 1940). The Super Putty Juic

at "make body plenty plastic" reveals the first bulges of the notion that gestated into Plastic Man eight months later.

a straight arrow—sort of a Boy Scout in some ways" as Gill Fox, Cole's close friend and his editor at Quality, described him to me.

Cartoonists "become" each character in their comics, acting out every gesture and expression; it's in this ontological sense that Cole most resembles Plastic Man—as the Spirit of Cartooning. Cole successfully performed the one magic act at the heart of the craft: believing so profoundly in the reality of the world conjured up with lines on paper that, against the odds, the marks gain enough authority to become a real world for the reader. Cole's world teems with invention, gags, and an amazing number of hyper-active characters tucked into every nook and cranny of a panel. Plastic Man never stretches exactly the same way twice. While Cole's work is often overloaded with ideas, the drawing is never overwrought; the art displays a Midwesterner's laconic mastery. What remains most remarkable is Cole's ability to be so fully present in his comic book work from moment to moment, always following his lines of thought with the same curiosity the reader might have—as astonished as any reader by where they take him.

If the standard going rate for pictures is still only a thousand words per, most *Plastic Man* panels are worth at least two or three pictures. Each panel seems to swallow several separate instants of time whole, as if the page were made up of small screens with different, though related, films whizzing by at forty-eight frames a second. Cole's is an amphetamine-riddled art: Tex Avery on speed! And it's not just Plastic Man who bounces and twists; any one of Cole's incidental figures would seem as kinetic as Plas if it were transplanted into someone else's comic book. Each page is intuitively visualized to form a coherent whole even though the individual panels form a narrative flood of run-on sentences that breathlessly jump from one page to the next. The art ricochets like a racquet ball slammed full force in a closet. Your eye, however, is guided as if it were a skillfully controlled pinball, often by Plastic Man himself acting as a compositional device. His distended body is an arrow pointing out the sights as it hurtles through time.

Panel detail, *Plastic Man* #17 (May 1949)

In just a single panel (opposite page, lower right), our hero chases along a footpath in a park, trailing a mugger. Running from the rear of the picture, Plastic Man's S-curved body echoes the path itself as he loops around one pedestrian in the distance and extends between two lovers about to kiss—lipstick traces are on his elongated neck as he passes them—to swoop up between an old man's legs like an enormous penis wearing sunglasses, and stare into his startled face.

Plastic Man had all the crackling intensity of the life force transferred to paper. Pulpier than James Cameron's Terminator, more frantic than Jim Carrey in *The Mask*, and less self-conscious than Woody Allen's Zelig, Plas literally *embodied* the comic book form: its exuberant energy, its flexibility, its boyishness, and its only partially sublimated sexuality. Cole's infinitely malleable hero, Clinton-like in his ability to change shape and squeeze through tiny loopholes, just oozed sex. It was never made explicit—the idea of a hard-core version

of *Plastic Man* boggles the mind—but there was a polymorphously perverse quality to a character who personified Georges Bataille's notion of the body on the brink of dissolving its borders. Cole let it all hang out as Plas slithered from panel to panel, sometimes shifting from male to female, and freely mutating from erect and hard boiled to soft as a Dalí clock.

Most of the plots are as twisted and swervy as Plastic Man himself. They're convincing enough in their mad, moment-to-moment flow, but they're as hard to reconstruct and as elusive as dreams with their vividly improvised incidents. Gender-bending and cross-dressing were the least of it. In *Police Comics* #5 Plas punches out the butchy Madam Brawn, a "kingpin" of crime, explaining that "I never strike a lady—but you're no lady!"—and then confesses his secret identity to her as she lies dying, pierced by a large spike she has fallen onto as a result of his blow. In another early story, Plas is swallowed whole by one Cyrus

"Plastic Man Products," *Plastic Man* #17 (May 1949). Above right and right: Plas as compositional device, steering one's eyeball around the page.

Police Comics #21 (August 1943)

IN THE CLUB, PLASTIC SEATS HIMSELF BESIDE HARDWICH

ICED TEA!

ICED WHAT?..

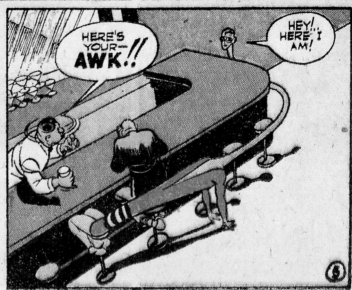

HERE'S YOUR—!! AWK!!

HEY! HERE I AM!

The humor in Plas's early 1940s stories stayed within a melodramatic mold (though Cole happily bent that mold out of shape). In "The India Rubber Man," for example, Plas tracks down a kidnapped industrialist and saves him from Madame Serpina's boa constrictor. *Police Comics* #21 (August 1943).

HURRY! PLAS!

LEMME GO!... YOU HEAR?

HELLLLP!

NO, NO, KIDS! SCHOOL'S NOT OUT YET!

GANGWAY!

UG!

BRUTE FORCE WOULD ONLY MAKE BOBO SQUEEZE TIGHTER... SO...

FREE! HOW'D YOU DO IT?

TICKLED HIS RIBS... FROM THE INSIDE!

Above: *Police Comics* #27 (February 1944). Right: *Police Comics* #24 (November 1943).

Smythe, a seventeenth-century mad doctor whose brain has been transplanted into a dying Army pilot's body. Smythe, who has learned how to grow hundreds of feet tall, but who must walk on his hands since the body he possesses is paralyzed from the waist down, chokes to death when Plas climbs out of his stomach to lodge himself in the giant's windpipe.

The early stories, while bizarre, don't feel psychopathic, sadistic, or even particularly mean-spirited in Cole's telling. In his postwar period the *Plastic Man* stories are totally nuts in a different way. They prefigure the early *MAD* comics, and owe more to the idea-per-minute vaudeville zaniness of Olsen and Johnson's *Hellzapoppin'* than to Krafft-Ebing's *Psychopathia Sexualis*. In all Cole's stories, heavily populated by shape-changing villains, mad scientists, and monsters, as well as by more mundane murderers, con men, and saboteurs, he demonstrates the termite go-for-broke quality that made his friend Gill Fox exclaim admiringly, "That's Jack—he'd let his mind go anywhere!"

10¢
A VITAL BOOK
PLASTIC MAN
IN THE
Game of Death!
4
Full Length
PLASTIC
MAN
Picture
Stories!
HE STREETCHES, SHRINKS AND BENDS!!

THIS IS NOT A PRETTY STORY!... ONE CAN HARDLY WRITE ABOUT THE ORPHAN, **WILLIE McGOON**, IN HAPPY PHRASES.... FOR POOR WILLIE- "THE GOON" IS CLASSMATES— LIVED IN CONSTANT GRIEF!!... TWENTY YEARS OLD AND STILL IN DE SCHOOL, HE WAS DERIDED FOR HIS IGNORANCE—THE TARGET OF EVERY MEAN K IN THE NEIGHBORHOOD.!! THOUGH STRONG AS A LION, WILLIE HAD NO TASTE REVENGE.!! HIS ONLY DESIRE IN LIFE WAS TO FIND, SOMEWHERE, SOMEHOW, RIEND..... **JUST ONE FRIEND !!!** WHAT HAPPENS WHEN THIS SIMPLE AMBITIO EALIZED, CREATES **THE MOST ASTOUNDING CASE IN THE CAREER OF** **PLASTIC MAN !!!**

In the postwar years Cole's zaniness got progressively more bent, precursing the wackiness of Harvey Kurtzman's early *MAD*.

By the late 1940s Cole was a virtuoso, telling stories in a manic language all his own and displaying a vivi vocabulary of exaggerated facial expressions and eloquently distorted body gestures that are shown from restless succession of angles and drawn in a style tha always takes chances but makes the goofy/graceful results look effortless.

These pleasures all inform November 1949's "Sadly-Sadly," reprinted in the pages that follow from *Plasti Man* #26. Every panel casually froths and brims over On page two, for example, in panel one, a medium shot, Plas eats a brown bag lunch while the FBI chief concentrates on a file, contortedly scratching his back in a gesture worthy of Plastic Man himself. Panel two, an extreme close-up of the chief's face mostly obscured by a speech balloon, shows a giant splash of tears landing on Sadly Saunders's dossier, announcing the theme played out in all that follows. In the next tier the chief absently reaches into the brown bag that rests on the "table" Plas's back has become. Plas sips milk through the straw his lips have become and Cole's "camera" pulls back for the next panel so that the emptied bottle can roll down his arm into a trash bin in the foreground.

Meanwhile, in that bottom row, the portly Woozy—concentrating on a newspaper casting call for sad-faced actors—is poured into a chair in a pose that only a limber five-year-old boy could manage and only Cole could draw. In the next panel, another extreme close-up, Woozy shoves his bulbous snout up against to a hand-held mirror and in the last panel the camera pulls back, appalled at what it sees, just like Woozy.

The reader turns to the next page to find Woozy twisting and turning as he weaves and bounces past dizzied bystanders and toward the reader. He career into a tightly knotted line of sad-faced mugs, and th ensuing chain reaction causes a mug in the middle to shoot up and out of the line like a cartoon banan squeezed out of its peel.

Hence starts Cole's rollicking Sadness Variations: the symphony of grief-stricken responses to Sadly Saunders's irresistible hangdog expression (no two responses mimed alike!) escalates into ever more risible moments and—climactically—into page 10's ugly mob attack on Plas, and page 11's mournful scenes of the crowd coming to its senses. The bigge their tears, the bigger the reader's yuks.

Cole's late 1940s work reveals him as a master at the top of his form. The only comic stories more manic are the totally over-the-top vaudeville turns of the very last Cole *Plastic Man* stories, those done in 1950, represented here by "The Plague of Plasti People" and the Woozy Winks "Dopi Island" yarn (both from *Plastic Man* #22, March 1950).

Left: A panel from "The City Was Starving on a Full Stomach," also from *Plastic Man* #22.

PLASTIC MAN
IT'S SADLY-SADLY SANDERS! DON'T LOOK AT HIS FACE, PLAS, OR YOU'LL BREAK DOWN AND LET HIM GET AWAY WITH ALL THIS STUFF!
WEARY WAY
MELANC ALLEY
SNIFF HE LOOKS SO SAD! MAYBE MY MONEY'LL MAKE HIM FEEL BETTER!
SOB SOB TAKE THEM, YOU POOR MAN! I CAN'T ENJOY WEARING THEM WHILE YOU LOOK SO WRETCHED!

PHIL SANDERS ...FORGER... SMUGGLER... BANK ROBBER... JEWEL THIEF! DISAPPEARED TWO YEARS AGO AND NO TRACE OF HIM SINCE!

DON'T RUB IT IN, CHIEF! I KNOW I LET HIM SLIP AWAY!

WHAT A FACE! IT ALMOST MAKES ME WEEP TO LOOK AT IT!

IT ALMOST MADE ME WEEP WHEN HE GOT AWAY!

CASE 16709-B PHIL SANDERS

IT WASN'T YOUR FAULT, PLASTIC MAN! I ONLY CALLED YOU IN AFTER THREE OTHER OPERATIVES HAD BUNGLED THE JOB!

THAT'S SMALL CONSOLATION!

SLURP! SLURP!

ANYWAY, IF HE'D PULLED ANYTHING IN THE LAST TWO YEARS WE'D HAVE HEARD ABOUT IT! HE'S CERTAINLY LYING LOW!

EVEN IN THE UNLIKELY EVENT THAT HE'S GONE STRAIGHT, HE STILL OWES THE LAW A DEBT AND HE'S GOT TO PAY IT SOMEDAY!

CLUNK

MEANWHILE...

"MARLOW CAMDEN, GENIUS DIRECTOR, SEEKS ACTOR TO FILL ROLL OF SAD CHARACTER! MARLOW SAYS FACIAL EXPRESSION MUST BREAK HEARTS OF AUDIENCE!"

HMM! A GUY'S FACE WOULD HAVE TO BE PRETTY AWFUL TO DO THAT!

ON THE OTHER HAND, PEOPLE HAVE OFTEN TOLD ME I HAVE A SAD FACE!

THERE'VE ALSO BEEN PEOPLE WHO'VE SAID WORSE THAN THAT ABOUT IT!

BUT IT SOUNDS LIKE AN EASY JOB IF I CAN GET IT!

I MAY BE ABLE TO BEAT THIS COMPETITION!

ALWIN THEATER

STAGE DOOR

A FINE THING! ALL BECAUSE OF PLASTIC MAN I'VE BEEN REDUCED TO HONEST ACTIVITIES FOR TWO YEARS!

THIS JOB MAY BE RISKY IF I GET IT! PLASTIC MAN MAY RECOGNIZE ME ON THE STAGE!

ALL RIGHT, GENTLEMEN, I'M READY TO LOOK AT YOU!

STILL, ACTING PAYS BETTER THAN MOST JOBS...AND WITH PLENTY OF MAKEUP I MAY EVEN FOOL PLASTIC MAN!

WHAT DO YOU THINK OF THIS FACE, MR. CAMDEN? IT ISN'T BAD!

IT'S BAD, ALL RIGHT, BUT IT ISN'T SAD!

3

NOW REPEAT AFTER ME! I... I'M BROKE... HUNGRY... STARVING!

I... I'M BROKE... HUNGRY... STARVING!

SADLY... SADLY! SAY IT VERY SADLY!

I... I'M BROKE... HUNGRY... STARVING!

OH... THE POOR GUY! THE POOR, POOR GUY!

HE'S BREAKING MY HEART! HE LOOKS SO PATHETIC! HE TALKS SO SADLY... SADLY!

HERE ARE MY LAST TWO BUCKS... ER... SADLY-SADLY! IT'S THE ONLY NAME I CAN THINK OF FOR YOU!

EVERYTHING WE HAVE IS YOURS! YOU MUST NEED IT WORSE THAN WE DO!

THEY'RE RIGHT! THE HAPLESS MAN IS PITIFUL!

SOB! SOB!

SOB!

TAKE IT! MY MONEY... MY WATCH... MY STICKPIN! I REFUSE TO OWN ANYTHING WHILE THERE'S SUCH MISERY ABOUT ME!

I'VE EVEN GOT HIM! WHAT AN ANGLE! I SHOULD WORK WHEN I'VE GOT THIS NEW GIFT FOR GETTING EASY DOUGH?

BOO HOO! SOB!

SLOBBER!

BLUB!

ALL I HAVE TO DO IS REMEMBER WHAT CAMDEN TAUGHT ME ABOUT THE TONE OF MY VOICE AND THE EXPRESSION ON MY FACE! I'LL BE ABLE TO PULL ANYTHING AND MAYBE EVEN WIN PLASTIC MAN'S SYMPATHY!

5

AN ARMORED CAR! WHAT AN OPPORTUNITY FOR MY FACE TO DO ITS STUFF!

STOP! LOOK AT THAT POOR GUY! THE LOOK ON HIS FACE IS BREAKING MY HEART!

MINE, TOO! HE'S THE SADDEST LOOKING GUY I'VE EVER SEEN!

≡SNIFF≡ IS THERE ANYTHING WE CAN DO FOR YOU? JUST NAME IT!

THE MONEY IN THE ARMORED CAR... YOU CAN HAND IT TO ME!

≡SOB≡ IT'S IMPOSSIBLE TO REFUSE HIM ANYTHING!

≡SOB≡ I CAN'T EVEN THINK ABOUT ANYTHING BUT HIS SADNESS!

YOUR CAR... I NEED IT!

YOU DON'T HAVE TO ASK ME TWICE! IF YOU WANT IT, IT'S YOURS! I'D RATHER DIE THAN SAY NO TO YOU! ≡SNIFF≡

GRAWK! WHAT HAVE WE DONE? WHAT CAME OVER US?

HOW COULD WE DO IT? WE WEREN'T OURSELVES... COULDN'T THINK RATIONALLY!

LET'S CALL THE POLICE AND CONFESS!

NO! I'LL CALL THE F.B.I.! THAT WAS AN INTERSTATE SHIPMENT!

WHAT? YOU COULDN'T HELP GIVING IT TO HIM BECAUSE HE HAD THE SADDEST FACE AND VOICE IN THE WORLD?

DID YOU HEAR THAT, PLAS?

THE SUBTLEST FORM OF HOLD-UP I'VE HEARD OF YET! I'LL GET TO WORK ON IT!

PLAS, CAN YOU LEND ME A FIN? I JUST GAVE MY LAST TWO BUCKS TO SADLY-SADLY WHILE I WAS TRYING TO GET AN ACTOR'S JOB!

SADLY-SADLY?

I NAMED HIM THAT AFTER MARLOW CAMDEN TOLD HIM TO LOOK AND TALK THAT WAY! WE ALL GAVE HIM OUR MONEY! WE COULDN'T HELP IT! CAMDEN EVEN FORGOT ABOUT THE PLAY UNTIL SADLY-SADLY WAS GONE!

HEY! THIS MAY BE SOMETHING! WHAT DID SADLY-SADLY LOOK LIKE?

WHY...ER...TERRIBLY SAD...LIKE...LIKE... GRAWK! LIKE THAT GUY... ONLY SADDER!

PHIL SANDERS! YOU WERE TAKEN LIKE THE ARMORED CAR...ONLY FOR LESS!

KONK!

WHAT'LL YOU DO, PLASTIC MAN?

I'VE GOT TO THINK! SADLY-SADLY...I MEAN PHIL SANDERS...ALWAYS WORKED AN ANGLE TO DEATH BEFORE HE QUIT!

7

HE'LL CONCENTRATE ON THE BIGGEST HAULS IN TOWN! LET ME SEE! IF I WERE SADLY, SADLY, WHAT WOULD I FIND MOST TEMPTING?

I GET IT, PLAS! YOU'RE GONNA SEE IF THE PAPER HAS SOME TIP-OFF TO A BIG JOB!

THIS MUST BE IT! NO CROOK WITH A HOT ANGLE WOULD PASS THIS UP!

TARTIER'S BUYS MAHARAJA OF DOMBOOR'S MILLION-DOLLAR COLLECTION OF JEWELS! ON DISPLAY TODAY!

BUT I'VE GOT A FEW ANGLES OF MY OWN!

PLAS! DON'T LOOK SADLY-SADLY IN THE FACE! IF YOU DO, YOU'RE SUNK! YOU'LL DO ANYTHING HE ASKS!

LATER, AT TARTIER'S...

THIS IS GOING TO BE LIKE TAKING CANDY FROM A BABY!

Tartier
MAHARAJA DOMBOOR JEWEL COLLECTION
ON DISPLAY TODAY

WH-WHAT IS IT, YOU POOR CHAP? IS THERE ANYTHING I CAN DO?

THOSE GEMS... IF I COULD ONLY TOUCH THEM!

MAHARAJA OF DOMBOOR JEWEL COLLECTION

:SNIFF: YES...YES... YOU CAN EVEN TAKE THEM IF IT'LL MAKE YOU FEEL BETTER! I CAN'T STAND SEEING YOU SO MISERABLE!

I MUSTN'T LOOK AT THAT FACE!

8

THANK YOU! I'M BEGINNING TO FEEL BETTER ALREADY!

YOU'RE GOING TO FEEL A LOT WORSE IN A MINUTE!

AWRK!

EXCUSE MY HAND ON YOUR FACE! I JUST DON'T WANT MY HEART BROKEN!

NO! NO!

GOODNESS! WHAT CAME OVER ME? I WAS ABOUT TO LET THE FELLOW TAKE THE JEWELS! NO WONDER THE BOSS HAD PLASTIC MAN ON THE JOB! THEY EXPECTED THIS TO HAPPEN!

LOOK! IT'S PLASTIC MAN!

HE MUST'VE NABBED A THIEF!

MRMPF! I'M NOT GIVING UP WITHOUT A FIGHT!

OUCH!

CRUNCH!

GOSH! LOOK AT THE POOR, SAD GUY! A MAN WHO LOOKS LIKE THAT CAN'T BE A CRIMINAL!

HE'S TOO PATHETIC!

9

:SNIFF: THAT PLASTIC MAN'S JUST A VICIOUS STRONG-ARM GUY!

THE BRUTE! HOW CAN YOU MEN STAND THERE AND LET HIM MAUL THAT MISERABLE MAN?

HEY! LET GO! YOU DON'T UNDERSTAND!

WE CERTAINLY DO, YOU MONSTER!

I CAN'T SHAKE THEM OFF! THERE ARE TOO MANY OF THEM!

BOY, THIS ALMOST MAKES ME LAUGH! BUT IF I LAUGH THE CROWD MIGHT STOP ITS GOOD WORK!

BOP!
CRASH!
SOB-SOB!

MOVING

BUT I WON'T REALLY LAUGH UNTIL I SEE YOU DEAD! WHAT A LAUGH I'LL HAVE THEN!

OHHH!

I'D BETTER BEAT IT BEFORE TARTIER'S CALLS THE COPS AND THEY START SHOOTING BEFORE THEY SEE MY SAD FACE!

WHAT ARE WE DOING? WHERE'S THAT SAD-FACED GUY?

HE'S GONE! WE MUST BE MAD! WE DON'T EVEN KNOW WHY WE'RE MAULING PLASTIC MAN!

GRRRR!
BAM!
CRUNCH!
BAM!

10

HE ISN'T MOVING!

HE LOOKS DEAD!

WE KILLED HIM WITHOUT KNOWING ANYTHING ABOUT THAT GUY WE WERE TRYING TO HELP!

WHEN I LOOKED AT THAT PATHETIC FACE I WAS READY TO DO ANYTHING FOR HIM, BUT NOW I DON'T KNOW WHY!

WHAT'S GOING ON?

WE'RE ALL GUILTY! WE KILLED PLASTIC MAN!

PLASTIC MAN DIES AFTER MAULING BY MOB! I HATE TO WRITE IT BUT IT'LL BE THE STORY OF THE CENTURY!

As EXTRA EDITIONS OF THE NEWSPAPERS APPEAR...

SO THEY REALLY DID IT! OH, BOY!

EXTRA! EXTRA! EVENING NEWS PLASTIC MAN DIES AFTER MAULING BY MOB! LIES IN STATE AT HOME

PLASTIC MAN DEAD! THIS I GOTTA SEE! I'M PERFECTLY SAFE GOING THERE, BECAUSE EVERYBODY'LL JUST FORGET PLASTIC MAN AND WEEP FOR ME WHEN THEY SEE ME!

GOT TO LOOK SAD SO THEY'LL START FEELING SORRY FOR ME AGAIN! GRAWK! I CAN'T MOVE MY MOUTH INTO A SAD EXPRESSION! PLASTIC MAN'S SOCK FROZE IT FOR ME!

I...I THOUGHT YOU WERE DEAD!

OBVIOUSLY! BUT AS MARK TWAIN ONCE SAID, THE RUMORS OF MY DEATH WERE GREATLY EXAGGERATED!

WHEN THE MOB HAD ME DOWN I HEARD YOU MAKE THAT CRACK ABOUT HAVING A GOOD LAUGH WHEN I WAS DEAD! I KNEW THAT IF YOU EVER LAUGHED I COULD GET YOU WITHOUT WORRYING WHAT YOUR SAD LOOK MIGHT DO!

SO I DECIDED TO PLAY DEAD ON THE CHANCE THAT YOU'D COME AROUND TO ENJOY YOUR LAUGH! YOU DID COME AROUND!

PLAS, BE CAREFUL! HE'S BEGINNING TO LOSE THAT GRIN!

WE'VE GOT TO DO SOMETHING! THAT SOCK ONLY FROZE HIS FACIAL NERVES FOR A FEW MINUTES! IF HE BECOMES SAD-FACED AGAIN HE MAY TALK US INTO LETTING HIM GO! I'VE GOT IT! HERE'S A FEATHER, WOOZY!

A FEATHER? OH, I GET IT, TOO, PLAS!

HAR! HAR! HAR! HAW! HAW! HAW! STOP IT! YOU'RE KILLING ME!

NOT A BIT! JUST KEEPING YOU AMUSED UNTIL WE GET YOU INTO A FOOR-WALLED CELL WHERE YOU CAN'T MAKE SAD FACES AT ANYBODY!

HO! HO! HA! HA! STOP IT!

HO! HO!

HAW! HA! HA!

IF I'D THOUGHT OF THIS BEFORE, I'D HAVE SAVED MYSELF PLENTY OF TROUBLE!

GULP! MY TERROR!

MY LUNCH!

WAIT TILL MY CONGRESSMAN HEARS ABOUT THIS OUTRAGE!

NOW WILL YOU TELL ME WHAT ALL THIS BRIEFCASE PEEKIN' IS ABOUT, PLAS? IT AIN'T LIKE YOU TO VIOLATE PEOPLE'S PRIVACY!

AN HOUR AGO SOMEONE HIT A BANK MESSENGER OVER THE HEAD AND WALKED OFF WITH A BRIEFCASE FULL OF BONDS! WE DON'T KNOW WHO!

WHAT DO YOU SUPPOSE MAKES PEOPLE DO THINGS LIKE THAT, PLAS?

SNAP!

APPLES ¢ LB.

PSYCHOLOGISTS TRACE IT TO A BASIC INSECURITY, WOOZY, STEMMING FROM AN UNHAPPY CHILDHOOD!

EASY, BOYS! ONCE WE MAKE THAT ALLEY, WE'VE GOT COVER CLEAR TO OUR HIDEOUT!

WILTON ST.

EEEOW! IT'S THAT PLASTIC PERIL AND HIS PUDGY PAL! FATE HAS DESERTED US!

MUGS MERKLE! FANCY MEETING YOU HERE, WEARING A STOLEN BRIEFCASE AND A GUILTY LOOK!

DO YOU MIND IF I JUMP TO THE CONCLUSION THAT MY SEARCH FOR THE MISSING BONDS IS AT AN END, MUGS?

YIII! DO SOMETHING, YOU DUMB DOPES!

SPLAT

THEY NEVER LEARN, DO THEY, PLAS?

NOT AT HIM, YOU HAMMERHEADS! IT'S THE FAT TWERP WHO AIN'T BULLETPROOF!

BANG! BAM! BANG! BAM!

2

HERE, HERE! YOU'LL HURT SOMEONE IF YOU AREN'T CAREFUL!

KEEP HIS HANDS OCCUPIED, BOYS! I JUST REMEMBERED AN URGENT ENGAGEMENT ELSEWHERE!

I DON'T NEED HANDS TO HANDLE YOU, MUGS!

STOP IT! THAT AIN'T SANITARY!

ADIOS, AMIGOS, AS WE USED TO SAY IN SING SING!

I'LL GET HIM, PLAS! NOBODY CAN CALL ME A FAT TWERP AND GO UNPUNISHED!

RIP!

PUFF! PUFF! COME BACK AND FIGHT LIKE A MAN!

AW, GO GET LOST, BUTTER-BALL!

FEAHH!! HELP, PLAS! I'M STUCK!

OH, FOR PITY'S SAKE! THIS IS CERTAINLY TURNING INTO A FOOLISH FIASCO!

A FINE BUSINESS! MUGS GOT AWAY WITH THE BONDS AND THERE'S NO WAY OF TELLING WHICH TUNNEL HE TOOK!

EITHER DIET OR STAY OUT FROM UNDER CARS, WOOZY!

CAN I HELP IT IF THEY BUILD THESE NEW CARS TOO CLOSE TO THE GROUND?

3

Later...

YOU'VE GOT TO FIND HIM, PLASTIC MAN! WHAT IF WORD LEAKED OUT THAT A DUMB HOOD LIKE MUGS OUTWITTED PLASTIC MAN?

I'LL FIND HIM, CHIEF! EVEN IF IT WAS A FLUKE, THE EFFECT WOULD BE DEVASTATING! AND THERE'S MY REPUTATION TO THINK OF!

CHIEF BRANNER

WAS IT TOUGH, PLAS? ANY IDEA WHERE TO ROUND UP THAT ROUNDER?

ER, YES, THERE IS, WOOZY! BUT YOU HAD BETTER STAY OUT OF IT! MUGS IS A DANGEROUS CHARACTER WHEN CORNERED!

F.B.I. CHIEF BRANNER

AW, PLAS, YOU KNOW I'M NO SOFTY! LEMME TAKE ANOTHER CRACK AT THAT VANISHING VAGABOND!

WEL-L-L, IF YOU INSIST! WE GOT A TIP MUGS MIGHT BE AROUND THE WATERWORKS LAGOON IN CENTER PARK, BUT I CAN'T GO THERE NOW!

SAY NO MORE, PLAS! I --- WILD-MAN WINKS --- WILL PERSONALLY PATROL THE PREMISES WITH A PEELED EYE!

GOOD! THAT GETS WOOZY OUT OF HARM'S WAY WHILE I CONCENTRATE ON THE TYPE OF DIVES MUGS FREQUENTS!

SWOOSH!

MEANWHILE, MANY BLOCKS AWAY ---

THE COAST IS CLEAR! I OUGHTA THANK PLASTIC MAN FOR NABBING MY MOB! NOW I DON'T HAVE TO SPLIT THIS LOOT WITH ANYBODY!

STEP RIGHT UP, FOLKS! RIGHT UP CLOSE, PLEASE, WHILE I DEMONSTRATE THE WONDERS IN THIS LITTLE BOTTLE!

NOW, WATCH CLOSELY, FRIENDS! FOR THE INSIGNIFICANT SUM OF ONLY A PALTRY FIVE DOLLARS...

ULP! FIVE DOLLARS!

? ?

ZIP!

SWISH!

WHIZZ!

ZIP!

4

WELL, IF IT AIN'T MY OLD PAL, PITCH PENNY!

MUGS MERKLE, AS I LIVE AND THIEVE! WHO YUH DOIN' THESE DAYS?

THE LANDLORD, MOSTLY! HOW'S WITH YOU?

IF BUSINESS GETS ANY WORSE, I MIGHT EVEN HAVE TO WORK!

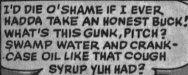

I'D DIE O' SHAME IF I EVER HADDA TAKE AN HONEST BUCK! WHAT'S THIS GUNK, PITCH? SWAMP WATER AND CRANK-CASE OIL LIKE THAT COUGH SYRUP YUH HAD?

NAW! IT'S LEGITIMATE... AND THAT'S WHY MY HEART AIN'T IN IT!

PITCH PENNY'S PATENT PLASTICIZER

IT'S JUST SOME KINDA STUFF THAT TURNS WOOD AND IRON AND JUNK LIKE THAT INTO RUBBER!

OH, IS THAT ALL IT... AWRRK!

YUH MEAN THIS STUFF'LL TURN AN IRON SAFE INTO RUBBER SO ALL YUH GOTTA DO IS STRETCH THE DOOR OPEN?

WELL, SURE! I NEVER TRIED IT ON A SAFE BUT IT SURE WILTED A COPPER'S GUN LAST WEEK!

I'LL TAKE IT... I'LL TAKE IT! YUH GOT ANY MORE? MAKE UP SOME!

ABOUT A GALLON LEFT AT HOME, I GUESS! BUT I CAN'T MAKE UP ANY MORE! THIS WAS KIND OF AN ACCIDENT, YOU MIGHT SAY...

I HAD A LOT OF OLD MEDICINE LEFT OVER SO I MIXED IT ALL TOGETHER! I WAS GONNA SELL IT FOR A COLD CURE--- BUT THIS IS WHAT I GOT! I DUNNO WHAT'S IN IT!

NOT THAT I DON'T TRUST YOU, OL' PAL, BUT LET'S SEE IT WORK ONCE!

5

WELL, THAT'S THAT! NONE OF MUGS' OLD ASSOCIATES HAVE SEEN HIM RECENTLY! I'D BETTER PULL WOOZY OFF HIS LONELY BEAT AND TRY SOME NEW TACTIC!

NO RIDERS

HMM! DID SOMEBODY SAY LONELY?

♪ TWEET ♪ TWEEOOO!

HI-YUH, BABE!

DAILY

HOW WOULD YOU LIKE DINNER ON THE VAN ASTORBILT ROOF, WITH CAVIAR, CHAMPAGNE, BREAST OF GUINEA HEN UNDER GLASS?

ULP!

OOO, YOU BIG, STRONG, HANDSOME HUNK OF MAN, YOU! BUT CAN YOU AFFORD A GORGEOUS DINNER LIKE THAT FOR JUST LITTLE ME?

WELL, NO...

BUT I GOT ENOUGH FOR TWO HAMBURGERS AT NICK'S DINER, HONEY!

DINER? WHY, YOU OVER-STUFFED OAF! DO YOU THINK I'M THE KIND OF A GIRL WHO'D GO OUT WITH A STRANGER?

DAILY PRESS

YEP! WE ALREADY ESTABLISHED THAT! NOW WE'RE DICKERING ON COSTS!

@@#*✕!?✕@! WOMEN ARE ABSOLUTELY UNPREDICTABLE!

HEY!

OOF!

PUBLIC WATER SUPPLY NO DUMPING NO SWIMMING

EEEAHHH!

WELL, WHY DON'T YOU LOOK WHERE YOU'RE GOING, STUPID?

PUBLIC WATER SUPPLY NO DUMPING, NO SWIMMING

YOU Col #*≠! CLUMSY TOAD! NOW LOOK WHAT YOU'VE DONE! I'M RUINED!

WHAT TH---?

YOU!

WAIT'LL I GET MY HANDS ON YOU! CALL ME NAMES AND STICK ME UNDER A CAR, WILL YOU!

GET BACK! LET ME ALONE OR I'LL BEAT BUMPS ON YOUR BEEZER WITH THIS BOTTLE! I'LL MELT YOU DOWN! I'LL---

MY GOSH! I WONDER IF THIS STUFF WOULD WORK THE SAME WAY ON PEOPLE! I NEVER THOUGHT OF THAT...

AH-HAAA! NOW I GOT YOU!

TAKE THAT!

WHOOOSH!

WHA---?

GONE! ALL GONE! MY BEAUTIFUL, LOVELY, WONDERFUL CRIME TOOL!

UH-OH! I THINK I JUST BETTER GO SOMEWHERE ELSE AND STAY THERE!

JUST A MOMENT, MY PUSSYFOOTING FRIEND!

I DON'T KNOW WHAT YOU'VE DONE BUT YOU'LL KEEP HERE UNTIL WE FIND OUT! SNEAKING OFF LOOKS MIGHTY SUSPICIOUS!

LEMME GO! I HAVEN'T DONE NOTHING! IT'S A FRAMEUP I TELL YUH!

YOU FAT WRECKER! IF IT WASN'T FOR YOU I COULD HAVE BEEN THE NAPOLEON OF CRIME! I'D HAVE RULED THE WORLD!

PUFF-GRUNT! I HOPE PLASTIC MAN CAN HEAR YOU! SAY THAT! SOMETIMES I THINK HE DOESN'T APPRECIATE MY HELP!

I HEARD IT, WOOZY! MAYBE I HAVE UNDER-ESTIMATED YOU! I'LL KNOW BETTER WHEN I GET TO THE BOTTOM OF THIS CRAZY SCRAMBLE!

YIIII! TAKE ME AWAY! NO-THING MATTERS NOW! MY WONDERFUL EMPIRE OF CRIME IS DUST AND ASHES, THANKS TO THIS CLUMSY CLOWN!

I THINK THEY'VE DROPPED A MARBLE SOMEWHERE, PLAS! ALL THEY DO IS YELL ABOUT MELTING VAULTS AND TURNING GUNS INTO RUBBER!

IT BEATS ME, WOOZY! WE'LL HOLD THIS OTHER FELLOW FOR INVESTIGATION TOO, AND--- ULP!

YIIIKE! WE'RE ALL PLASTIC--- LIKE PLASTIC MAN!

MA, LOOK WHAT I KIN DO!

EEEK!

HEY, PLASTIC MAN--- LOOK! WE'RE ALL OF A SUDDEN JUST LIKE YOU! WHO DO WE SUE?

BELIEVE ME, I'M AS SHOCKED AS YOU ARE BY THE WHOLE THING! I---JUST A MOMENT!

YOU WERE YELLING ABOUT TURNING THINGS INTO RUBBER! LET'S HAVE THE STORY!

YIII! LET ME DOWN! I'LL TALK! I'LL TELL EVERYTHING!

A FEW MOMENTS LATER---

AND THAT'S THE HONEST TRUTH, PLASTIC MAN! PITCH DON'T KNOW WHAT WAS IN THE STUFF AND IT GOT DUMPED IN THE LAGOON!

IN THE CITY WATER SUPPLY? THIS IS HORRIBLE! WE'VE GOT TO DO SOMETHING RIGHT AWAY!

CHIEF, SOMETHING TERRIBLE'S HAPPENED! THE CITY WATER'S FULL OF STUFF THAT MAKES PEOPLE PLASTIC LIKE ME! YOU WON'T BELIEVE IT, BUT---

WHAT MAKES YOU THINK I WON'T BELIEVE IT?

GET OUT, WOOZY! THIS IS PRIVATE F.B.I. BUSINESS WE'RE DISCUSSING!

YOU, TOO? CHIEF, WE'VE GOT TO CUT OFF THE WATER, IMPORT PURE WATER AND TRY TO ANALYZE THE STUFF AND FIND AN ANTIDOTE!

CHIEF BRANNER

EXCUSE ME, BUT I PASS HERE EVERY DAY AND I'VE OFTEN WONDERED WHAT WENT ON INSIDE! MIND IF I PEEK OVER YOUR SHOULDER?

YES, WE DO! GET OUT!

SHOULD I OR SHOULDN'T I? I COULD BE A REAL HELP TO PLAS IN HIS CRIME FIGHTING! BUT ON THE OTHER HAND---

I TELL YOU, CHIEF --- WE'RE HEADING TOWARD MADNESS!

F.B.I. CHIEF BRANNER

PRIVATE

10

AW, T'HECK WITH IT! HERE GOES! SLURP-SLURP!

I WONDER HOW IT FEELS TO BE PLASTIC! OOF! OOF! WELL, WHY DON'T I STRETCH LIKE THE OTHERS DO?

MAYBE I DIDN'T DRINK ENOUGH! I'LL TRY--- EEOCK! THE DRINKING FOUNTAIN TURNED TO RUBBER---BUT I DIDN'T!

BWAAA! I WANNA STRETCH, TOO!

COME ALONG, WOOZY! WE'VE GOT TO TRY TO HALT THIS WAVE OF TERROR THAT IS SWEEPING THE CITY!

ULP! DID YOU SAY WAVE OF TERROR, PLAS?

THIS IS ONLY THE FIRST STAGE! THE TERROR WILL COME WHEN CRIME CATCHES ITS BREATH!

I DON'T UNDERSTAND IT, BUT WHO CARES? I'M LEAVIN'!

CELL BLOCK 6

GORY STORY

OH, NO YOU AREN'T, LOUIE! SIT DOWN AND BEHAVE YOURSELF OR I'LL SEND YOU TO THE RUG FACTORY!

YUKKK! NO, NOT THAT! ANYTHING BUT THAT!

GORY STORY

GET DOWN TO THE SEVENTH NATIONAL, PLASTIC MAN! SOMEBODY'S JUST WRIGGLED THROUGH THE KEYHOLE IN THE VAULT DOOR!

ULP! RIGHT AWAY, CHIEF! COME ALONG, WOOZY!

FBI

ONE SIDE, PLEASE! LET US THROUGH...

WE WANNA GO ALONG!

WE WANNA WATCH YOU OPERATE SO WE CAN BE PLASTIC CRIME FIGHTERS, TOO!

WE'RE AS GOOD AS YOU ARE NOW!

NEVER MIND, PLASTIC MAN! HE LEFT AGAIN WHEN HE FOUND HE COULDN'T SQUEEZE MONEY OUT THROUGH THE CRACK IN THE DOOR!

IF THIS KEEPS ON YOU'LL HAVE TO REDESIGN THE WHOLE BANK!

VAULT

PRESIDENT

SOMETHING MUST BE DONE... BUT WHAT?

UB BLUB

BLUB

BLLLP! IT'S NO USE! I'VE DRUNK GALLONS OF CITY WATER AND STILL I CAN'T STRETCH!

HOLD EVERYTHING! HERE COMES THE POLICE CHEMIST, ALL EXCITED!

WE FOUND TRACES OF A RARE SUBSTANCE IN THE WATER, PLASTIC, BUT IT DISAPPEARED BEFORE WE COULD ANALYZE IT! NOW IT'S ALL GONE!

HOORAY! MAYBE THE STUFF EVAPORATES IN A LITTLE WHILE! LET'S CHECK WITH THE CHIEF!

BEAH!

CHIEF! WE'VE GOT GOOD NEWS! CHIEF, WHERE ARE YOU?

HAL-LP! GLUG-GUG! HALP!

ULP!

YEEEK! HE'S BLOWN HIS TOP AND IS COMMITTING SUICIDE!

12

CHIEF, WHAT ON EARTH ARE YOU DOING UP HERE?

GET ME DOWN! I WAS LOOKING TO SEE IF THE CLEANING WOMAN DUSTED UP HERE...AND ALL OF A SUDDEN I LOST ALL MY STRETCH!

WONDERFUL! THEN THE STRETCHABILITY DRUG WEARS OFF IN A LITTLE WHILE AND PEOPLE WILL GO BACK TO NORMAL! THANK GOODNESS!

YOU'RE RIGHT, PLAS! THEY'RE ALL NORMAL OUT HERE---AND SORE AS BOILED OWLS ABOUT IT!

AND I KNOW HOW THEY FEEL! DOGONNIT, NOW I'LL NEVER KNOW HOW IT WAS TO BE PLASTIC!

WHAT A ROUNDUP, PLASTIC MAN! ALL THE KNOWN CRIMINALS GOT CAUGHT WHERE THEY DIDN'T BELONG WHEN THEIR ELASTICITY WORE OFF!

ALL WE HAVE TO DO IS LOAD THE WAGONS!

I'D LIKE TO KNOW WHY I DIDN'T STRETCH! EVERYBODY ELSE DID... AND I DRANK SO MUCH WATER I'M SICK!

WE DON'T KNOW MUCH ABOUT PITCH'S PLASTICIZER, WOOZY, BUT I THINK WE CAN ANSWER THAT QUESTION...

DRINKING THE WATER WITH THE DRUG IN IT HAD NO EFFECT ON ANYBODY, SO FAR AS WE CAN DETERMINE! THE ONLY ONES IT AFFECTED...

---WERE THOSE WHO BATHED IN IT!

ULP! ER---AW--- IT WASN'T SATURDAY NIGHT, ANY HOW!

WOOZY

GOSH, IMAGINE ME, WOOZY WINKS, BEING A KING! WHEN WILL I GET CROWNED?

IMMEDIATELY, YOUR HIGHNESS!

MAYBE I SHOULD HAVE TOLD PLASTIC MAN I WAS COMING HERE TO OOPI ISLAND FOR A VACATION! CRIME BUSTING IS GETTING ON MY NERVES!

VERICOSE LINES

THIS IS WHAT I NEED--PEACE AND QUIET! NO EXCITEMENT, NO CROOKS, NO GUNFIRE---

ZIP

BANG!

YEOW! I SPOKE TOO SOON!

PIZ

PLASTIC MAN

COME WITH US! YOU'RE THE ONLY MAN IN THE WORLD WHO CAN GET US OUT OF THIS MESS!

WE KNEW IT THE MINUTE WE LAID EYES ON YOU!

HEY, NOW, WAIT A MINUTE! I OFFERED TO HELP BUT I WANT TO KNOW WHAT I'M BEING DRAGGED INTO! I DEMAND AN EXPLANATION!

SURE! WE'LL BE GLAD TO TELL YOU!

YOU'RE GOING TO BE KING OF DOPI ISLAND!

HUH? DID YOU SAY KING?

YES AND THERE'S NO TIME TO LOSE! THE SOONER YOUR NOBLE SELF ASCENDS THE THRONE, THE MORE RELIEVED WE'LL BE!

THAT'S YOUR CASTLE AHEAD!

GOSH, IMAGINE THAT! MY FRIEND PLAS WILL SURE BE SURPRISED WHEN HE HEARS THAT I'M A KING! HEH, HEH!

GEE, I'VE GOT QUITE A JOINT HERE, HAVEN'T I?

YOU AND HIS HIGHNESS WAIT HERE, ROOK! I'LL GO AND...ER...PREPARE FOR THE CORONATION!

PRICE $9,000.25

KING REGINALD, I'VE COME TO ADVISE YOU ON A MATTER OF GRAVE IMPORTANCE!

MAKE IT SNAPPY! YOU KNOW AFFAIRS OF STATE BORE ME!

MINK MILK

THE PEOPLE KNOW YOU'VE ROBBED THEM! THEY DEMAND REPAYMENT BY SATURDAY OR THEY'RE GOING TO RUB YOU OUT!

WHAT? YOU MEAN THEY'RE GOING TO ASSASSINATE ME? GRAWK!

3

YOU AND ROOK GOT ME INTO THIS! YOU SAID I COULD SWINDLE THE BUMS AND GET BY WITH IT!

RELAX, REGGIE! THERE'S NOTHING TO WORRY ABOUT!

THERE'S A DOPE OUTSIDE NAMED WOOZY WINKS! HE'S A DEAD RINGER FOR YOU! WE'LL MAKE HIM KING AND LET HIM GET BUMPED OFF!

HOT DOG! THE SUBJECTS WILL THINK I'M DEAD AND BE SATISFIED! AND I'LL STILL HAVE THE DOUGH!

I CAN STILL BE RICH AND NOT HAVE TO BE KING ANYMORE! YIPPEE!

PIPE DOWN SO HE WON'T HEAR YOU! WE DON'T WANT HIM TO GET WISE!

GIVE ME YOUR CLOTHES! THEN YOU LOCK YOURSELF IN THE CELLAR UNTIL THIS WINKS GUY'S DEAD AND IT'S SAFE TO MAKE A GETAWAY!

BOY, THIS IS A LOAD OFF MY SHOULDERS!

SPARE NOTHING FOR THE JERK'S ENJOYMENT! WE WANT HIM TO BE HAPPY TILL SATURDAY!

LEAVE IT TO ME! HE'LL LOLL IN LUXURY!

SO, FOR THREE DAYS...

GOSH! WHO'D EVER THOUGHT LITTLE OLD WOOZY WINKS WOULD COME TO THIS?

ARE YOU COMFORTABLE, YOUR HIGHNESS?

CHOMP CHOMP GOLLY, THIS IS GOOD!

THE CONDEMNED KING EATS HEARTILY!

LIKE A PIG!

4

"-- AND SO THE KING WENT BACK TO HIS CASTLE AND LIVED HAPPILY EVER AFTER!"

THAT'S THE BEST BEDTIME STORY I EVER HEARD! HO, HUM!

THEN CAME SATURDAY... BRING ON THE DANCING GIRLS! I HAVEN'T GOT ALL NIGHT!

HE DOESN'T KNOW THE TRUTH OF HIS WORDS! THE ASSASSIN MAY STRIKE AT ANY MINUTE!

LET ME THROUGH! I DEMAND TO SEE THE KING!

HERE I AM! COME IN! THE MORE THE MERRIER, I ALWAYS SAY!

DON'T BE FUNNY! WE WANT OUR DOUGH! THIS IS YOUR LAST CHANCE!

GEE, BOYS, I'M A LITTLE SHORT! ALL I HAVE ON ME IS A DIME!

OKAY, YOU CROOK! YOU ASKED FOR IT!

HEY, WATCH WHAT YOU'RE DOING! SOMEBODY COULD GET HURT THAT WAY! AND DON'T CALL ME A CROOK!

BANG!

YIEEE! LET ME OUT OF HERE!

STOP SHOOTING! I CAME HERE FOR A REST!

BANG!

BANG BAM BAM BAM

JEEPERS, THEY ACT LIKE THEY'RE OUT TO GET ME! HEY, PLAS! HELP!

BANG! BANG!

BANG! BANG!

PLASTIC MAN!

WHAT'S THIS ABOUT PLASTIC MAN?

READ THIS HEADLINE, YOU IDIOT! NOW WE'RE REALLY IN A MESS!

$BAM!

"WOOZY WINKS IS MISSING! PLASTIC MAN BEGINS WORLD-WIDE SEARCH! SWEARS VENGEANCE IF HARM HAS COME TO--" GRAWK!

IF HE FINDS OUT WE'RE RESPONSIBLE FOR GETTING HIS PAL POPPED OFF, WE'LL ALL HANG!

WH-WH-WHAT'LL WE D-D-DO?

THERE'S ONLY ONE THING! SIGH! GIVE THE PEOPLE THEIR DOUGH! I'D RATHER BE A POOR HONEST KING THAN A DEAD ONE!

HELP!

BANG!

C-C-CEASE F-F-FIRING! HERE'S YOUR MONEY!

THAT'S WHAT WE WANT!

IT'S ALL WE ASKED FOR!

G-GOSH! FOR A WH-WHILE I TH-THOUGHT THEY WERE M-MAD AT ME. NOW MAYBE I CAN RELAX AND ENJOY BEING K-KING!

OH, NO! YOU'RE GETTING OUT OF HERE FAST! I MEAN, YOUR TERM OF OFFICE IS OVER! THAT'S THE WAY WE DO THINGS ON DOPI ISLAND!

YEAH! HERE'S YOUR HAT! WHAT'S YOUR HURRY? GOOD-BYE!

ZIP!

OF ALL THE GOOFY CUSTOMS! I'M GOING BACK TO CRIME BUSTING! IF A GUY STAYED AROUND THIS PLACE VERY LONG, HE'D BE A NERVOUS WRECK!

FOUR

Gill Fox told me that he remembers starring in an eight-millimeter home movie that Cole shot some time in the early 1940s, after Jack and Dorothy became his neighbors in Stamford, Connecticut, in order to be closer to Quality's studio there. Cole's improvised film scenario, about an ambitious, young comic book artist fighting a deadline, had Fox dragging his drawing table into the bathroom, pulling his pants down, and continuing to work while seated on the toilet. Cole was always behind schedule, a procrastinator and a perfectionist who took pride in his craft and managed to turn out his monthly quota only by working for punishing all-night stretches. Fox recalls a sweltering summer day in the Quality studio that has become legendary among his generation of comic book artists: only the nasty buzz of horseflies broke the silence of cartoonists sweating at

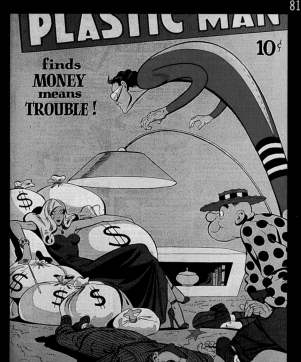

their desks over some exceptionally brutal deadline, until a disturbance broke their concentration. Something was fluttering and streaking by above their heads. All work stopped until they caught what turned out to be one very angry horsefly hauling a long tissue paper banner with the words "Drink Pepsi Cola!," which Cole had patiently lettered and glued to the insect's back. A genius at work!

Above: "Money means trouble!" *Plastic Man* #16 (March 1949).

Left and below: A handmade Christmas card from Jack and Dot to his family in New Castle during the war years.

Creig Flessel, an intimate colleague of Cole's, visited the Quality offices around that time, wanting to observe an old letterer there who could ink in text balloons perfectly without pencilling. He noticed "Busy" Arnold with large scissors at a nearby desk cutting old *Plastic Man* originals to ribbons: "I nudged Jack and pointed it out to him, and he just shrugged sheepishly." After the art was used, Arnold routinely destroyed it to prevent unauthorized reprinting. The disposability of the art was a given, but it makes Cole's pride in his craft seem downright existential!

The pressure to produce lots of pages quickly, in a situation that offered little prestige and relatively small rates for the skills involved, took its toll. "A number of the artists I knew back then cracked," says Fox. "Al Bryant, who drew Doll Man, drove himself into an abutment on the Long Island Expressway shortly after a nervous breakdown. Another guy at Quality, a writer, threw himself in front of a subway, but somehow survived." John Spranger, an exceptionally gifted artist who assisted on Plastic Man in the postwar years, had a severe breakdown; Bob Wood, like many of the other artists, drank heavily. It was a tough business, making funny books, but Cole flourished in that environment.

At the start of World War II, Cole doubled his workload to put money aside for Dorothy in case he got drafted. Although he never had children, and was apparently in good health, he wasn't taken. He wisecracked to friends that he'd worked himself too ragged to be fit for service. As one of the best cartoonists left on the home front at a moment when publishers

Above: Detail from "Mr Aqua," Plastic Man #25 (September 1950).

TO BE CONTINUED IN #2

were selling all the comics their newsprint rations let them print, Cole made out well. He even briefly ghosted the daily newspaper version of *The Spirit* when Will Eisner got drafted. By the end of the war, Cole was getting the top rate for comic books (about $35 per page) as well as occasional bonuses of up to $2,500 when his books broke the 200,000 point. He and Dorothy bought property and settled into a series of houses in New England. "Their Stamford place was a fourteen-room mansion that had once belonged to the Masked Marvel, a famous pool shark," Flessel told me. "Dorothy

Above: Detail from "City of the Future," *Police Comics* #48, (November 1945).

Left: *Police Comics* #23 (October 1943). Though Plas was the starring act in *Police Comics*, Eisner's approach imbued the entire Quality line of comics, and his weekly *Spirit* stories—originally done as comic book supplements for newspapers—were reprinted in *Police Comics* from the tenth issue on.

Far left: Three 1942 *Spirit* daily strips (from the back cover of a 1971 Dutch reprint, with logo and color added by Joost Swarte). The war year dailies, ghosted by Cole, were scripted by Manly Wade Wellman and Jules Feiffer.

was horrified by the cold marble tiles when she first saw the house, so Jack put in some wall-to-wall carpeting. It must have set him back plenty, but he absolutely doted on his wife." Flessel remembers Cole with great affection as an acute, thoughtful, and gentle guy, "a pussycat," with a screwy smile and an irrepressible streak of humor. When I visited the Flessels' Long Island home, he conjured up one small Jacques Tati–like moment when the Coles were leaving after a weekend visit there in the mid-forties: stooping to get behind the wheel of his pint-sized car, the oversized Cole knocked his homburg to the ground. He scooped it up while shutting the car door, then casually put the hat back on top of the roof and drove off waving.

Cole worked at home, sending in his popular fifteen-page lead stories for *Police Comics* every month, as well as material for his *Plastic Man* solo title and occasional humor pieces for other comics. Fox has said,

Perhaps *The Spirit* and *MAD* have been more celebrated than *Plastic Man* simply by being more readily available in reprint form. Cole provides the "missing link" between Will Eisner's sensibility and Harvey Kurtzman's.

Some of Kurtzman's earliest pre-*MAD* work, "Flatfoot Burns," appeared in *Police Comics* in the 1940s. Looking back at his homage to Plas ("Plastic Sam," *MAD* #14, August 1954), Kurtzman admitted that it was hard to parody a parody. (Sigh. It all would have been a lot funnier if rendered by Kurtzman's best collaborator, Bill Elder, who shared Cole's sense of excess, rather than by Russ Heath's perfunctory reworkings of Kurtzman's breakdowns.)

In one sequence, Plastic Sam disguises himself as a beautiful girl's tight-fitting red coat (*hubba! hubba!*). Kurtzman thereby acknowledges the sexual subtext that always oozes through Cole's work.

In "Plastic Sam" Kurtzman, a satirist, points out that a soft and pliable man would have teeth too rubbery even to chew gum; Cole, a fantasist, made the point that in comics anything one could dream one could draw.

Plastic Man #2 (August 1944)

by JACK COLE

"Jack insisted on doing everything himself. . . . He didn't even clear his plot lines with anyone. The only thing we did was copy-read for mistakes." Cole was elated to get his own book; but when he was told that it would mean having assistants and ghosts do some of the stories, he burst into tears. (Neither Flessel nor Fox could verify what might be an apocryphal story, but both independently said it sounded like the Cole they knew.) The problem of Cole's ghosts and assistants plagues anyone who admires his work. Since some of his assistants—most notably his worshipful friend Alex Kotzky and John Spranger—were very skillful mimics, as schooled as Cole in the Quality house style, and since Cole didn't always sign his own art, the "forgeries" are sometimes as hard to spot as Plastic Man himself in disguise. When the characters tilt and sway, unable to hold themselves upright at a mere ninety degrees, when

Above: Plas does a double take in *Plastic Man* #21 (January 1950). Below: Woozy weighs in, from *Plastic Man* #22 (March 1950

Above: Plas as ticker tape in *Plastic Man* #22 (March 1950). Below: *Plastic Man* #17 (May 1949).

GHOSTS!

Top: Panels from "Dr. Volt," *Plastic Man* #7 (Winter 1947). The art has Cole's bounce and vigor . . . but isn't by Cole. Gil Kane (an authority on such matters) speculated that it was by John Spranger, a talented Quality artist who went on to draw *Don Friday* and *The Saint*.

Above: Kane wasn't keen on his own attempts to revive Plas for DC Comics in 1966.

A fragment of a Plas story from *Police Comics* #98 (February 1950) by Alex Kotzky, Cole's most able assistant. From 1961 until his death in 1996 Kotzky drew the gracefully rendered soap-opera strip *Apartment 3G*.

that extra blaze of invention—a few more ideas than any sane artist would dare squeeze into a panel—shines through, one can surmise one is in the hands of the master. *Plastic Man* was totally ghosted after 1950, when Cole reached his giddiest heights before burning out on the character. The ghosts who remained behind lost their inspiration, but the buoyant originality of the basic concept kept *Plastic Man* afloat through 1956. Subsequent attempts to revive the character haven't been especially distinguished, nor have imitations that recycle the notion of a stretchable hero, though the character's virtual DNA lives on in the leader of Marvel Comics' Fantastic Four, a "straight" Plastic Man with way too much starch.

IMITATION PLASTIC

If none of Cole's ghosts were able to deeply inhabit Plastic Man, DC Comics' occasional attempts to do so since the 1960s (with art by Joe Staton, Ramona Fradon, and others) have also fallen flat. DC even tried its own spin on a stretching hero, The Elongated Man, who made his debut in *The Flash* in 1960 (see panel by Ernie Chua, below). The elegance of the Carmine Infantino-inflected house style that delineated this minor character was oddly inappropriate for the concept.

Right: Jack Kirby's Mister Fantastic—a Plastic Man with far less snap?

Bottom: Though the filmmakers may have been more aware of Tex Avery than Jack Cole, Jim Carrey's The Mask catches some of Cole's antic energy.

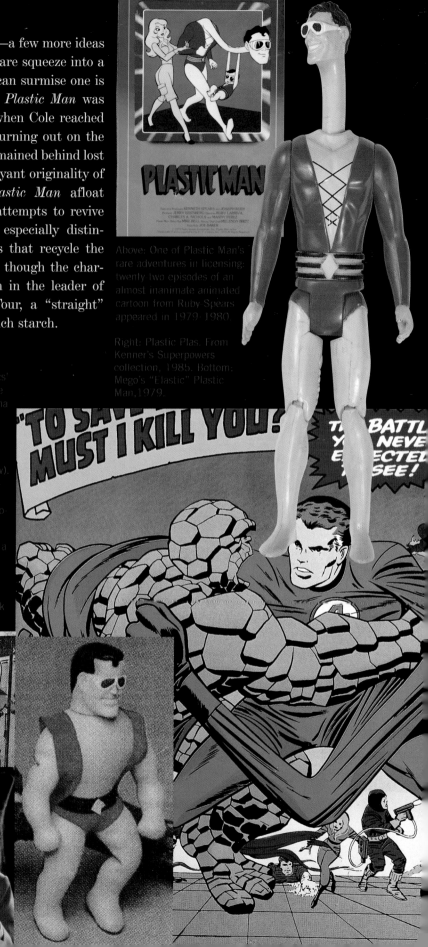

Above: One of Plastic Man's rare adventures in licensing: twenty-two episodes of an almost inanimate animated cartoon from Ruby Spears appeared in 1979-1980.

Right: Plastic Plas. From Kenner's Superpowers collection, 1985. Bottom: Mego's "Elastic" Plastic Man, 1979.

"TO SAVE YOU MUST I KILL YOU?"

THE BATTLE YOU NEVER EXPECTED TO SEE!

I'M OFF TO LOOK INTO THIS MIRROR MYSTERY, HONEY...

REMEMBER, RALPH--THAT'S *MY* MIRROR! DON'T LET *ANYTHING* HAPPEN TO IT!

I'M SO SORRY TO DISAPPOINT YOU!

PERHAPS YOU WOULD PREFER TO MEET SOMEONE WHO LOOKED LIKE THIS?

SIGHHH! DON'T WAKE ME UP --- JUST LET ME DREAM!

OR WOULD YOU LIKE ME TO LOOK EVEN MORE MENACING? I CAN DO IT, YOU KNOW!

GHAAA!

P-P-P-PLAS! I THINK HE M—

I KNOW OKAY, B

PAGE 34   PLASTIC MAN

WHAT, Y'MEAN TO SAY YOU BEEN LIVIN' HERE FIVE HUNDRED YEARS?

WHY NOT? ... YOU'LL DO THE SAME! ONCE WE GET IN HERE, WE'RE MADE OF THE SAME STUFF AS THE VOLCANO!

HOLY SMOKE! YOU'RE RIGHT! I AIN'T ME ANY MORE! I'M MADE OF—

LAVA, SEÑOR! MOLTEN LAVA! YOU MAY AS WELL GET USED TO IT!

BUT I DON'T WANNA STAY DOWN HERE! I GOT THINGS TO DO! I GOTTA GET OUT!

PERSONALLY, SEÑOR I WOULDN'T LEAVE FOR ANYTHING!... I LIKE IT HERE! BUT IF YOU INSIST ON GOING, YOU MAY LEAVE ON THE NEXT STREAM OF LAVA THAT SHOOTS UP TO THE MOUTH OF THE VOLCANO

CRIPES! LOOK! – I GOT THREE LEGS... NO, FOUR! AND I FEEL LIKE I CAN HAVE TEN IF I WANT 'EM!

SI, SEÑOR! YOU CAN DO ANYTHING WITH YOUR BODY NOW! IT'S POSSIBLE TO PUT IT INTO ANY SHAPE! NOW IF YOU WISH TO LEAVE, YOU HAVE MERELY TO SIT IN THE POOL OF LAVA THERE!

WELL, WHEN DO I GET GOIN'?

SOON NOW ... BUT YOU WILL BE BACK! HEH! HEH! YOU'LL RETURN AND BE GLAD TO STAY HERE WITH ME!

YIPE!

MY ARM! ... IT'S BEEN KNOCKED OFF!

A MERE TRIFLE, SEÑOR! SPROUT SEVERAL NEW ONES! IT'S EASY!

SAY! IT IS EASY! LOOK! ... I GOT TWO OF 'EM!

In 1947 Cole hired Alex Kotzky to help him package *True Crime Comics,* a new publisher's short-lived attempt to cash in on the crime comics then dominating the field; a story in the second issue, "Murder, Morphine and Me," has become notorious as one of the most intense and delirious examples that the lurid genre had to offer. One small panel—so charged that it has tremor lines around it and tilts, almost tumbling off the page—was enshrined as Exhibit A in Dr. Fredric Wertham's *Seduction of the Innocent,* the book that triggered the Senate hearings and thereby toppled the industry: it shows a close-up of Mary Kennedy, the dope-dealing protagonist, being stabbed in the eye by a junkie with a hypodermic needle. I concede that this isn't Mother Goose, but I find the panel (part of a dream sequence, incidentally) emblematic of the comic book's visceral power to pass the reader's analytical defenses and pierce the brain. Dr. Wertham, on the other hand, focused on the depraved image as an example of "the injury-to-the-eye motif . . . [that] shows perhaps the true color of crime

Above: That eyeball-popping panel from *True Crime Comics* #2.

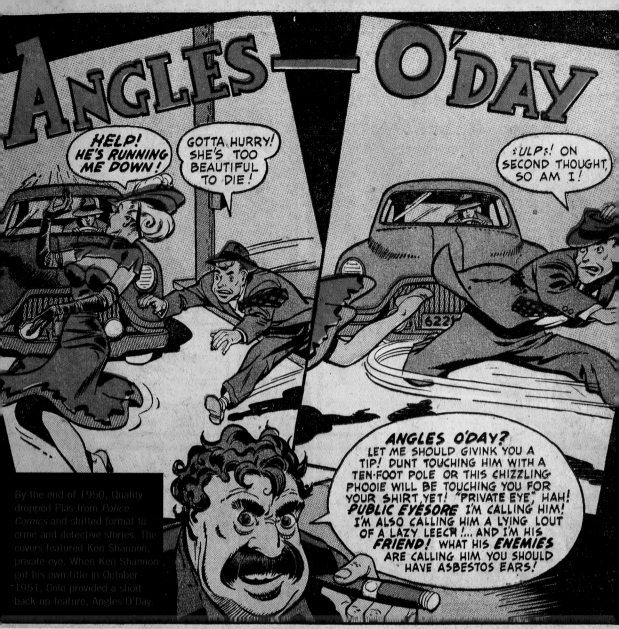

comics better than anything else. It has no counterpart in any other literature of the world, for children or adults." I suspect that Dr. Wertham never saw Luis Buñuel and Salvador Dalí's *Un Chien Andalou* (the 1929 film shocker that featured a close-up of a woman's eye getting slashed by a razor), but that it had made a strong impression on Cole. On the other hand, Cole's *True Crime* capers point out the continuum between Cole's manic humor and plain old mania. As Kotzky recalled, "Jack was a wild man mentally."

The New York State Legislature thought enough of "Murder, Morphine and Me" to reprint eight pages of blow-ups and excerpts in its 1951 report on comic books and censorship. As a young teen in the arid comic book landscape of the early sixties, I stumbled onto this report in Manhattan's Donnell Library. It was my first exposure to Cole, and I checked the report out repeatedly. The story included ethnically stereotyped Scandinavians and Italians, lingerie shots of Mary Kennedy, and more gangland gunplay than there is in a John Woo Hong Kong action flick, all delivered with Cole's signature velocity. It is also among the most formally sophisticated comics stories I've ever seen; all the elements, including the panel shapes and the lettering, are deployed for narrative effect. When Mary, working as a hash slinger, first spills coffee on Tony, seated at her lunch counter, it's love at first sight. Through two progressive close-ups, moving from profiles of their faces to their twitching lips, they exchange a machine-gun volley of speech balloons with dialogue worthy of James M. Cain. Tony departs ("Be seein' ya, honey eyes"), leaving Mary almost swooning, her heart banging against her chest like a five-

hundred-pound canary trying to break out of its cage. (Cole's body language is priceless.)

Cole's last comic book work was for *Web of Evil*, Quality's entry into the horror comics that put the final nails into the industry's coffin. Unlike most of his output, these horror comics, often scripted and barbarically inked by others, look as if they were done for the money. One noteworthy tale,

What a hell of a place to carry your fish hooks… in your hip pocket!

clearly by Cole, "The Killer from Saturn," is about a serial murderer from outer space who terrorizes the city but turns out to be a mousy municipal window clerk who has gone postal. Wearing an imposing monster costume and stilts, he takes revenge on those who abused him. He's put in a mental institution where, in the closing panel, two detectives outside the barred door peer in at the pathetic wimp who still insists he's the omnipotent killer from Saturn. One cop says, "He always will be . . . up

here . . . where he can safely kill . . . in his imagination." The story, laced with fifties psychological jargon, seems to be Cole's hymn to the power of fantasy and the need to keep that power contained.

If Cole was through with comics, comics were also through with him. Searching for work in the fifties, he is said to have brought his portfolio to DC Comics, one of the few publishers that survived past 1954, and was summarily turned away. As early as the mid-forties, Cole had been preparing to leave the field, more out of ambition and restlessness than remorse. He began to put much of his energy into reshaping himself as a gag cartoonist, selling occasional drawings to *The Saturday Evening Post,* *Collier's,* and *Judge.* A knack for drawing genuinely sexy women made his cartoons, often signed "Jake," a regular fixture of the down-market girlie-cartoon and pin-up magazines.

Cole was struggling as a mid-echelon gag cartoonist at the end of 1953, when he submitted a batch of gags to *Stag Party,* a planned men's magazine that announced its need for cartoons in trade journals. Cole's drawings began appearing in the fifth issue of the magazine, after it was launched as *Playboy.* At least one full-page drawing by him appeared in *Playboy* every month thereafter for the rest of his life.

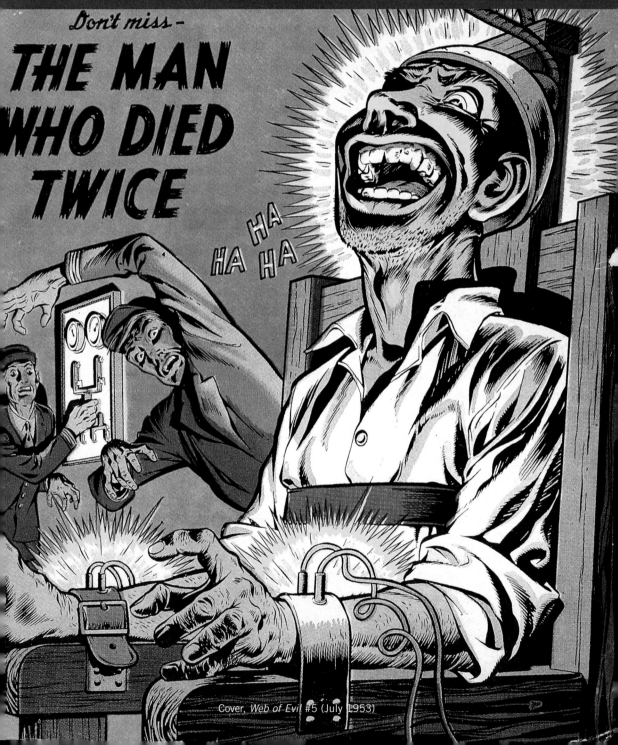

Cover, *Web of Evil* #5 (July 1953)

Left: A beautifully mapped out and typically overcharged page from "Meet the Split Benny Wilson" in *True Crime Comics* #3.

Bottom left: By the early 1950s the Jake cartoons had become a regular fixture of the girls-and-gags magazine circuit.

Below: Cole began selling cartoons to *Judge* very early in his career. By 1946, looking for new worlds to conquer, he began trying his hand at a series of Petty girl–style pinups (*Judge*, January 1946).

Right: In 1947 Cole edited and packaged *True Crime*, one of the many crime comics that followed in the blood-soaked trail of the trendsetting *Crime Doesn't Pay* comic edited and published by cronies from his earliest days in the field. The notorious "Murder, Morphine and Me," reprinted on the following pages in its entirety, appeared in his first issue.

"Really, your honor, when I started my law suit, I didn't expect you for a suitor."

JUDGE

I told you the barn is next door to the right!

WHY AM I TELLIN' YOU ALL THIS? I DUNNO... EVER GLIM THE FACE OF A DRUG ADDICT? IT DOES SOMETHIN' TO YA! THE HORRIBLE, GAUNT MASK OF YELLOW....EYES SUNK DEEP IN THE SKULL HOLES, SUCKIN' TH' SKIN INTO WRINKLED WHIRLPOOLS OF AGONY! Y' JUST DON'T FORGET PICTURES LIKE THAT! TAKE THAT EVENIN' IN L.A. FRINSTANCE......

MARY! YOU'VE GOT TO HELP ME! WON'T LAST THE NIGHT IF I DON'T GET MORE—MARY!! WAKE UP!!

G'WAY! LEMME DIE! SEE YA INNA MORNIN...ZZ

PLEASE, MARY! I RAN SHORT TODAY! BEEN CALLIN' YOUR NUMBER EVERY HOUR.. BUT NO ANSWER!! TONY, THAT LIAR, SAID YOU'D LEFT TOWN! WHY THE BRUSH? YOU CAN'T DROP ME NOW! YOU'VE GOTTA TRUST ME!

OH...YOU! (YAWN) TONY MUST BE SLIPPIN', LETTIN' A SICK HOPPY JUMP HIM FOR MY ADDRESS...AND LATCH-KEY! LIKE I SAID BEFORE, NO CASH. NO DOPE!

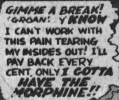

GIMME A BREAK! 'GROAN' Y' KNOW I CAN'T WORK WITH THIS PAIN TEARING MY INSIDES OUT! I'LL PAY BACK EVERY CENT, ONLY I GOTTA HAVE THE MORPHINE!!

WE'VE TRIED YOUR WAY BEFORE, HOPHEAD! ONE NEEDLE-FULL OF JOY-JUICE AND YOU GET SO SATISFIED WITH THE WORLD YOU FORGET YOUR OBLIGATIONS! NO, WE'LL DO IT MY WAY FOR A CHANGE!

YOU SLIMEY LEECH! I'VE LOST MY HOME, MY WIFE, JOB—EVERYTHING! TRADED THEM IN FOR A LOUSY SHOT IN THE ARM! A LITTLE RELIEF FROM THE AGONY THAT SCREAMS FOR MORE AND MORE! AND NOW, AFTER YOU'VE BLED ME DRY, YOU TELL ME.....

OKAY! OKAY! THERE'S A PACKAGE BEHIND TH' DRESSER-HELP Y'SELF! I'LL SQUARE IT WITH THE BIG BOSS SOMEHOW!

YES, MARY KENNEDY.. YOU TRY TO SQUARE THINGS WITH THE BIG BOSS!

P-PUT TH' NEEDLE DOWN!!.. NO!

OLESON! VOT DAT VAS?? IT SOUND LIKE JANE!

STOP SHAKING AND GET UP! SHE'S MAYBE NIGHTMARES HAVING!

BURGLARS MAYBE! YIGGERS! MY GUN.... AY BANE LEFT IT DOWNSTAIRS!

GOD BLESS OUR HOME

YOU ALLRIGHT, JANE? NO-LIKE AY SAID, SHE'S DREAMING TINGS AGAIN!! OH, DEAR!

WAIT'LL TONY COMES! HE'LL FIX—DON'T DO IT! I'LL...I'LL...

TCH, TCH!

THUD!

2

THERE IS ONLY ONE TRUE CRIME COMICS — THIS IS IT!

TONY! TONY!! HELP!!

NO, IT'S ME—OLIE YOHNSTON! YOUR FRIEND!!—MAMA, YOU TELL HER! YOUR VOICE SHE LIKES!

NO TIME FOR TALKING... TIME FOR GRABBING QUICK BEFORE SHE YUMPS!

??? M-MRS. JOHNSTON! WH-WHAT ARE YOU DOING IN A RACKET LIKE THIS?.... OH... ER... SORRY!.. I THOUGHT—

SUCH DREAMS, YOU POOR TING!...HERE...TIME AY PUT UP CLEAN CURTAINS ANYVAY!... THAT OLIE!.. ONCE HE SAW A MOVIE MAN THROW VATER ON FACE OF GIRL WHO VAS OUT OF HER HEAD—NOW EVERYBODY GETS A BATH

AY TANK AY FIX JANE SOME HOT TEA!

GEE...I MUSTA BEEN PRETTY ROUGH!.. DID I...AH... SAY ANYTHING?

NOW, YUST FORGET DREAMS AND THIS TONY SOMEBODY! HOT TEA FOR THE NERVES AND YOU BANE SLEEP BETTER, YA?

WH-WHAT'S TH' USE? IT ONLY COMES BACK AN' BACK AN' BACK! :SOB:

JANE, DEAR... EVER SINCE YOU COME TO ROOM HERE, YOU SAY NOTHING, BUT AY SEE! MAYBE NOW YOU LIKE TO TALK?... SOMETIMES IT HELPS, TALKING!

WHEN I THINK OF IT I HAFTA LAUGH! IT WAS GONNA BE SO EASY!... ALL'I HADDA DO WAS CHANGE MY NAME AND ADDRESS AND START OFF FRESH... LEAVE MARY KENNEDY, KANSAS CITY—THE WHOLE MESS— AND WALK AWAY CLEAN!... HAH!! WOULDN'T TONY LOVE TO SEE HIS BROKEN-DOWN MOLL, NOW! YEAH, WE'D BOTH HAVE A GOOD YUK! :SOB:

THE FEDERAL BUILDING IN KANSAS CITY IS TH' LAST PLACE YA'D EXPECT T'MEET A GANGSTER, IT WAS THAT CRAWLING WITH G-MEN! BUT THEY WERE LIKE NUTHIN' TO TONY PETRILLO! HE USTA BRASS RIGHT INTO PAPA DONNICI'S RESTAURANT, THERE, AN' JUST SIT— NOT SAYIN' A WORD— STARIN' AT ME!! HE'D GET ME SO WEAK IN THE KNEES I COULD HARDLY SERVE...

PAPA, IF YOUR SON CAN WHIP UP FORMULAS LIKE YOU CAN COOK, HE'S A CINCH FOR THE CITY CHEMIST'S SPOT! HOW'S FOR SOME PIE?

MARY, FIXA PIE FOR MIST' INSPECTOR!

AH, JOSEPHI, HE'SA WAN BUSY BOY! YOU SEE HOW MUCH BETTER THE CITY WATER, SHE'SA TASTE SINCE THEY MAKE HIM ASSIST-CHEMIST? ATSA MY JOE! ALLA TIME HE'SA WORK HARD!

YES, PAPA— OH!... I-I'M SO SORRY!

HERE... LET ME! GEE, HOPE IT DOESN'T LEAVE A SPOT! GUESS I WASN'T WATCHING WHAT I....I...

THE MAN'SA WAIT FOR HIS PIE, MARY!

THERE IS ONLY ONE TRUE CRIME COMICS — THIS IS IT!

THERE IS ONLY ONE *TRUE CRIME COMICS* — THIS IS IT!

THERE IS ONLY ONE *TRUE CRIME COMICS* — THIS IS IT!

THERE IS ONLY ONE *TRUE CRIME* COMICS — THIS IS IT!

THERE IS ONLY ONE **TRUE CRIME COMICS** — THIS IS IT!

THERE IS ONLY ONE *TRUE CRIME COMICS* — THIS IS IT!

THERE IS ONLY ONE **TRUE CRIME COMICS** — THIS IS IT!

THERE IS ONLY ONE *TRUE CRIME COMICS* – THIS IS IT!

THERE IS ONLY ONE _TRUE CRIME COMICS_ — THIS IS IT!

THERE IS ONLY ONE _TRUE CRIME COMICS_ — THIS IS IT!

THERE IS ONLY ONE **TRUE CRIME COMICS** — THIS IS IT!

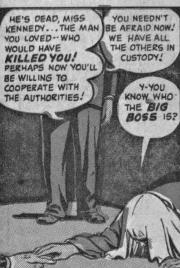

THERE IS ONLY ONE *TRUE CRIME COMICS* — THIS IS IT!

FIVE

Hugh Hefner had grown up reading and loving *Plastic Man* and, in a phone interview, described it to me as "the most hallucinogenic comic book of its time." At first Hefner didn't realize that he was working with *that* Jack Cole; indeed, the deft and sophisticated gag cartoons that appeared in *Playboy,* often in confidently applied, rich watercolor, bore almost no stylistic resemblance to Cole's brash comic book art. Hefner remembers receiving the first submission, and though there was nothing he could use in that first batch, he said,

"I loved the free and loose line, the quality of even those first pencil roughs, and I wrote a letter strongly encouraging him to send more. One of the things I tried to do was, like *The New Yorker,* develop a stable of artists closely associated with my magazine."

Cole soon signed an exclusive contract with *Playboy* and, in effect, became its defining artist—its Peter Arno. *Playboy*'s first art editor, Art Paul, told me, "Cole helped give the magazine its visual identity. Unlike Gardner Rea and Eldon Dedini, who came from *Esquire,*

"I ain't got no bod-eee..."

One of the voluptuous —in every sense— watercolors that helped establish Cole as *Playboy*'s definitive cartoonist in the 1950s. From the January 1958 issue.

MAN ABOUT THE BEACH

IN RECENT ISSUES, PLAYBOY has devoted entirely too many pages to pictures of pretty girls. A man enjoys viewing an occasional well-built male torso, too: witness the popularity of the profusely illustrated men's body building, health and strength magazines. So we sent artist Jack Cole to the beach with instructions to bring back sketches of the most interesting masculine musculature he could find. It's just possible we sent the wrong man. At any rate, on the next four pages are the best of the drawings he made, along with some explanatory notes by the artist.

I FOUND THIS PERFECT SPECIMEN FLEXING HIS MUSCLES NEAR THE WATER— MORE BULGES THAN A CHRISTMAS STOCKING — MIGAWD, WHAT A CHEST. STATISTICS: 48" — 10"— 10½" (THE 48" IS PLENTY HAIRY). GENERAL COMMENT: PAINTING CONDITIONS POOR — BEACH VERY CROWDED — OTHER BATHERS KEPT GETTING IN THE WAY WHILE I WAS SKETCHING.

Cole was a *Playboy* product." In fact, Females by Cole cocktail napkins were the second product *Playboy* licensed, right after the cuff links based on Paul's famous rabbit logo. The Females, horny derivations of William Steig's symbolic drawings, were breezy black-and-white brush impressions of women's psychological states. Cole came up with the concept for the ongoing feature; Hefner, as the very hands-on cartoon editor, worked closely with him. A self-confessed failed cartoonist, Hefner had actually drawn and toyed with publishing his own "Tijuana Bibles," hard-core cartoon parody booklets, shortly before he came up with the tonier *Playboy*, and Hefner's own drawings appeared in the magazine's earliest issues "until I could afford better."

In 1955, on his first trip to New York after launching *Playboy*, Hefner visited Cole's home in New Milford. The Coles had just resettled there after floods destroyed their house in Winsted, Connecticut, laying waste to most of their furniture and possessions. Hefner urged Cole to move to the Midwest, and he reluctantly agreed. He wrote to Gill Fox, "Middle of January the boss is moving us to Chicago. Swore I'd never leave these old hills, but he's dangled so much green bait what're you going to do? The sad part is leaving old friends. . . . But it's the biggest pile of eagle-shit that ever landed on us, so I'm gonna grab a fork and wade in." Although Hefner offered Cole a staff job, he preferred to work at home, and, at the beginning of 1956, settled into what he called that "pool table of a state," buying a place in the town of Cary, Illinois, about forty miles northwest of Chicago. Hefner was twelve years younger than Cole, and yet, he told me, "My heroes were now working for me—but as Cole's editor, of course, I was the father figure."

Cole's popularity led Richard Prather, a hard-boiled detective writer, to describe a character in one of his paperbacks, *Strip for Murder*, by evoking Cole: "She looked like one of Cole's

Above: Part of a five-page color feature, "Man About the Beach," *Playboy*, July 1955.

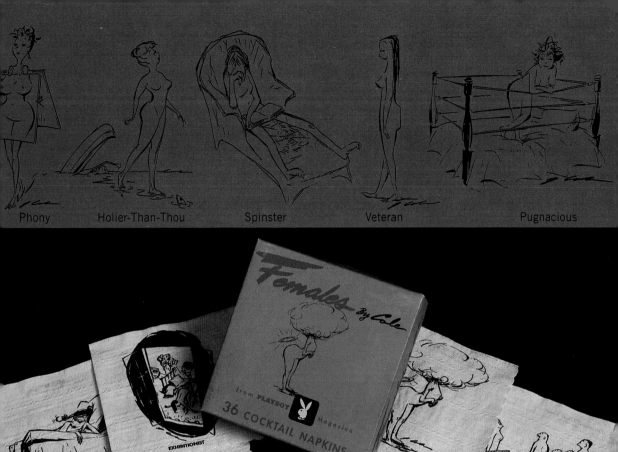

Phony   Holier-Than-Thou   Spinster   Veteran   Pugnacious

Cole drew over fifty "Females" for *Playboy*. In an introduction to a 1965 book collecting them all, Hugh Hefner described these as "psychograms.... A wickedly gallant salute to the vagaries of the delightfully opposite sex."

Craven   Starlet   Curious   Hypocrite   Fragile   Pro

Above: *Betsy and Me,* Cole's vaguely autobiographical fantasy in daily installments.

sensual women in *Playboy* magazine—blonde, with big brown eyes and those other big things you hear about but don't often see. At least don't often see so well. Not often enough, anyway." Hefner points out that Cole was still drawing fantasies for *Playboy.* Cole's goddesses were estrogen soufflés who mesmerized the ineffectual saps who lusted after them. The stacked nightclub chanteuse who sings "I ain't got no bod-eee . . ." in one of his oft reprinted color cartoons makes Marilyn Monroe, whom she's modeled after, look hard-boiled. Cole had climbed to the top of the heap in comic books, even if he looked back on it as a dung heap; now he was the star cartoonist for the hottest and hippest "slick" in America.

In the hierarchy of the applied arts, the comic book has been near the bottom—above only tattoo art and sign painting—and every commercial artist has been as aware of these unspoken aesthetic ranks as any American who isn't white has been of race. The gag cartoon, being a self-contained, single-image composition and therefore a distant cousin of painting, has been seen as more worthy. The comic strip—because of the fame and great fortune it can bring, and because this is America, where such things have mattered most—has been at the pinnacle. Early in 1958, unbeknownst to Hefner, Cole drew up several weeks worth of a newspaper strip called *Betsy and Me,* and walked the samples over to Field Enterprises' Chicago Sun-Times syndicate after a meeting at *Playboy.* Cole, like Plastic Man, had changed his appearance: *Betsy and Me,* drawn in the

then ultramodernistic, *Gerald McBoing-Boing* minimalist fifties style, looked like nothing he had done before. The complex ongoing "voice-over" narration by Chester Tibbet, the nebbish husband, about family life with his wife, Betsy, and their five-year-old boy genius, Farley, actually has a formal connection to the inventive narration in "Murder, Morphine and Me." The mature verbal sophistication Cole demonstrates in *Betsy and Me* may be a by-product of the cultivated milieu he encountered through *Playboy.* The syndicate knew nothing about Cole's other careers, but found the feature fresh and exciting. The strip was launched that May and was appearing in nearly fifty newspapers by the summer; the forty-three-year-old cartoonist's childhood ambition for a successful strip of his own was finally being realized.

Then Cole snapped.

"Like they say in the travel folders, Miss Duncan — 'Getting there is half the fun.'"

"I have it: let's swap wives."

Playboy, June 1955

Playboy, May 1958

...ase Monday, June 9, 1958

...SY AND ME

By Jack Col...

...WHERE WAS I?... ...H YES—THE BLESSED ...VENT! WELL SIR, BY ...EORGE, RIGHT ON' ...CHEDULE—POW!! ...HINGS HAPPENED SO ...AST, I'M A LITTLE ...UZZY ON THE ...DETAILS....

...BUT BETSY SAID I WAS A GREAT HELP TO HER...

WHERE IS THAT CAB?!

EASY, BETSY! WHERE'S THE BLUE CROSS?

HERE'S YOUR CAT AND HOAT!

...SHE COULDN'T HAVE MANAGED WITHOUT ME...

S-STEADY! WATCH THAT CIGAR BUTT!

STAND BACK!! AIR! AIR!!

HOT WATER—JUST IN CASE—!

...BETSY SAID THE THING THAT COMFORTED HER MOST WAS MY CALMNESS UNDER FIRE...

LADY, I GOT SOME SMELLING SALTS....

DON'T YOU DARE!

BUT, THEN, WHAT'S A HUSBAND FOR, BUT TO LEAN ON?

CITY HOSPITAL

6-9

...se Tuesday, June 10, 1958

...Y AND ME

By Jack Cole

...ACED AND PRAYED AND ...T AND DOZED! FINALLY ...E NURSE COMES OUT ...AND WHISPERS....

IT'S A BOY

BUT I HEAR IT LIKE....

IT'S A BOY!

6-10

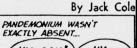

PANDEMONIUM WASN'T EXACTLY ABSENT...

MY SON! MY SON!

MY LAUNDRY!

ROOKIE!

COLE

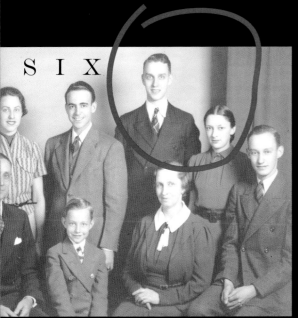

SIX

On Tuesday evening, August 12, 1958, Cole went to a party at *Playboy*'s offices. According to Hefner's private journal, Cole "was seemingly in the best of spirits." Art Paul told me that Cole, who was habitually temperate, drank a bit more than usual at the gathering, and seemed somewhat overexcited. Cole told him he had something he needed to say—the art editor found this exceptional, since they weren't intimate, and work-related issues tended to be taken up directly with Hefner—but someone interrupted, and the conversation never took place. The next morning Cole greeted a neighbor, a railroad conductor he'd known since moving to Cary, who noticed nothing out of the ordinary. At around 2:00 P.M., Cole told Dorothy he was going out for the mail and the papers. He took their Chevy station wagon, and at around 5:00 showed up at Dave Donner's Sport Shop in nearby Crystal Lake. He bought a .22-caliber, single-shot Marlin rifle. Between 5:15 and 5:30 he phoned the same neighbor he'd seen earlier and, after apologizing for the imposition, asked him to tell Dorothy he was going to end it all. Then he hung up. At around 6:00

P.M., on a gravel road a few miles from his home, three boys found Cole slumped behind the wheel of his car: a bullet wound in his head, the rifle in his lap, and a note on a tablet next to him. He was still alive. At 6:10, a McHenry County deputy sheriff, who had been notified of the suicide threat, showed up. The deputy called an ambulance but Cole died in the hospital at 6:45 P.M. without having regained consciousness. Cole's note read, "To whom it may concern: Please notify my dear wife, Dorothy Cole, 703 Silver Lake Road, Cary, Illinois, but first tell a neighbor so someone will be with her when she receives the news. Thank you. Jack Cole. Please forgive me, hon." Cole's body was carried back to New Castle and he was buried there on August 16.

On the day he killed himself, Cole had mailed two letters, which were received the next morning; one was to his wife, the other was to Hugh Hefner. The letter to Hefner reads:

AUG 13 '58

DEAR HEF:

WHEN YOU READ THIS I SHALL BE DEAD
I CANNOT GO ON LIVING WITH MYSELF
& HURTING THOSE DEAR TO ME.
WHAT I DO HAS NOTHING TO DO WITH
YOU. YOU HAVE BEEN THE BEST GUY
I'VE EVER WORKED FOR IN ALL THESE
YEARS. I'M ONLY SORRY I LEAVE, OWING
YOU SO MUCH, BUT DEAR DOROTHY WILL
REPAY YOU WHEN THE ESTATE IS SETTLED
I WISH YOU NOTHING BUT THE BEST
IN THE YEARS TO COME.
ALSO, MY BEST REGARDS TO PAT, ART,
RAY, JOE, ETC. ETC. & ALL THE OTHER
FINE FOLKS AT PLAYBOY.

THANKS AGAIN FOR EVERY THING, HEFFER.
YOU'RE A GOOD BOY.

Kindest regards,
Jack

stopper of a corpse. It also drives a thin wooden stake of rational explanation through the corpse's heart—to punish the dead for their rebuke to the living. The handful of people who care about Cole or his work have speculated as wildly about his suicide as any school class puzzling over E. A. Robinson's chestnut, "Richard Cory," that poem about another enviable gentleman who "one calm summer night / Went home and put a bullet through his head." Baseless rumors about money problems, terminal illness, sub-

At the inquest, the coroner asked Dorothy about the letter Cole sent to her. She testified that in it he explained why he had killed himself. The coroner was able to establish that Cole had never been under a doctor's care for any nervous condition and then asked Dorothy if she knew of any reason he may have had for taking his life. Dorothy answered only, "We had had an argument before." When a juror asked if the letter would be entered as evidence, the coroner said, "The letter was a very personal letter. I read it myself. We just wanted to bring it out that far." After Cole's death, Dorothy did not maintain contact with her husband's family or friends. Hefner, too, lost track of her, though he knows that "she remarried about a year or so after."

Speculating about a suicide's motives at least keeps a dialogue alive with that conversation-

stance abuse—more plots than could fill a *True Crime* comic book—have hovered over Cole's death. Did he suffer from manic-depression? Cole was never diagnosed, but, like Plas, he had his ups and downs. Dick Cole recalls that as a young man his brother once came home furious after an argument with his fiancée, Dorothy, his hands all bloody from pummeling every tree he'd walked past. Insofar as these things run in families, Cole's uncle, his father's brother, Frank, had a breakdown and committed suicide a short time after Jack moved to New York. Cole's association to *Playboy*, especially, has fueled prurient gossip about swinging affairs and infidelities. When I asked Hefner if Cole took part in the *Playboy* lifestyle, he chuckled: "He was no Shel Silverstein." If Cole's last letter to Dorothy had some sordid confession or salacious details, they remain unknown since the coroner, Theron Ehorn, was no Kenneth Starr. As a result of his discretion, the big question marks that hang over all suicides can't be dispelled with much more precision than to say that something had gone wrong in the Coles' twenty-four-year-long marriage and Jack Cole blamed himself. As Hefner told me, "It's an unresolved mystery. His end is as inconclusive as a Somerset Maugham story."

Above: *Police Comics* #76 (March 1948)

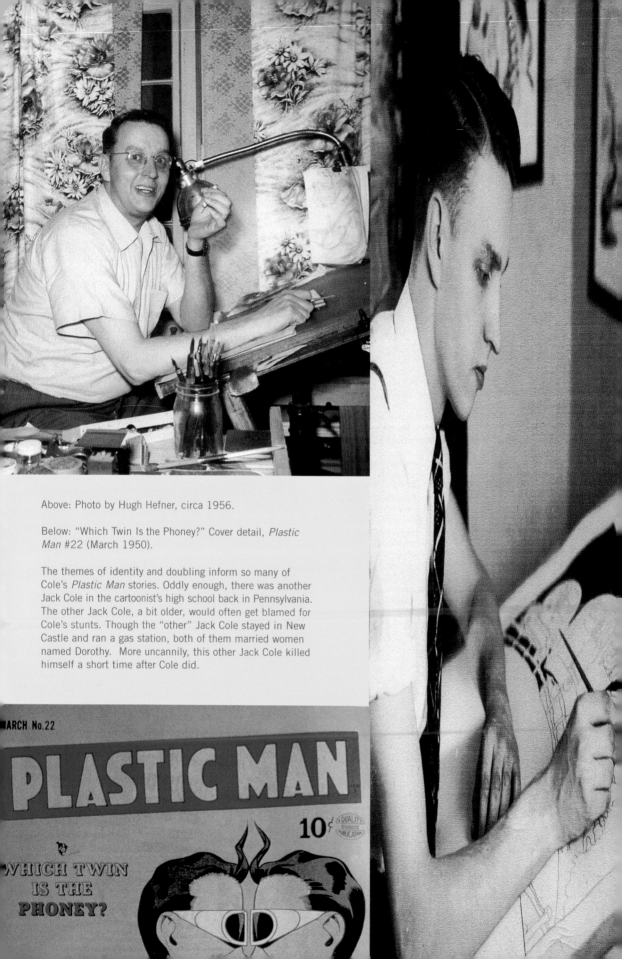

Above: Photo by Hugh Hefner, circa 1956.

Below: "Which Twin Is the Phoney?" Cover detail, *Plastic Man* #22 (March 1950).

The themes of identity and doubling inform so many of Cole's *Plastic Man* stories. Oddly enough, there was another Jack Cole in the cartoonist's high school back in Pennsylvania. The other Jack Cole, a bit older, would often get blamed for Cole's stunts. Though the "other" Jack Cole stayed in New Castle and ran a gas station, both of them married women named Dorothy. More uncannily, this other Jack Cole killed himself a short time after Cole did.

MARCH No. 22

PLASTIC MAN

10¢

QUALITY COMICS PUBLICATION

WHICH TWIN IS THE PHONEY?

Opposite page: *Playboy*, January 1956.
A surprising number of Cole's *Playboy* cartoons are
about impotence and loss.

Below: An old gent looks down on young lovers, Cole's
melancholy last cartoon for *Playboy*, July 1959.

Was Cole "unbalanced"? Of course, it goes with the suicide's job description. Jacques Rigaut, a Dada artist who shot himself in 1929, once said that "suicide is a vocation"; it's at least one hell of a career move—look at Sylvia Plath!—and it turns one toward an artist's work as if to a career résumé. "The mystery of his death informs the work," as Hefner put it. Suicide does indeed figure in many of Cole's comic book stories, like 1949's "Mr. Morbid," wherein a criminal perfumer concocts an essence of misery (one whiff and you knock yourself off), but most of Cole's cronies used suicide as a plot device without going on to self-destruct. More to the point may be the astonishing number of his *Playboy* cartoons that have impotence as their subtext. Putting aside limp jokes about Plastic Man's inability to get it up, impotence—or, rather, the psychologically linked issue of potency as the power to conceive a child—was key to Cole. All who knew Cole told me that he doted on kids and would have made an exceptionally good father. Jack and Dorothy's childlessness cast a poignant shadow on their isolated lives.

Hefner, who still misses the man and his work, has published several reprint tributes to Cole over the years. One *Playboy* classic shows a middle-aged milquetoast stretched

out on an analyst's couch. "In the beginning," he recounts wistfully, "I created the heavens and the earth. . . ." Although Cole looked back on his own beginnings in the comics with disenchantment, dismissing the "comics mags" in a letter to a friend as being "for the birds," he did have the power to soar and create worlds there, with barely an editor to shackle him.

Plastic Man was a stream of consciousness, allowing Cole's id the license to ooze freely, and in its bounces and lurches Cole found grace and balance. When he traded in Plastic Man's silly putty for *Playboy*'s silicone, he also traded away the innocent and omnidirectional sexuality of infancy for the mere heterosexuality of adolescence. Sublimating further, he squeezed his creativity into ever smaller boxes: his two-dimensional newspaper strip is as sexless as any other 1950s sitcom. Cole's heartbreaking "fantasy" about a loving couple doting on their brilliant little boy—it reads like a suicide note delivered in daily installments! As he climbed his ladder of success, up from the primal mulch of the comic books, he finally arrived at air that was too thin to breathe: Jack Cole, a comics genius, died of growing up.

"In the beginning, I created the heaven and the earth..."

Mr. McCabe had been ...
...nce the attack.

For the past year he was
...ost concerned over the mys-
...rious disappearance of his as-
...ociate, Amelia Zelko. Miss Zel-

Jack Cole, Comic Strip Creator, Shot To Death

Jack Cole, 43, creator of
comic strip, Betsy and Me, was
found shot through the head
Wednesday night in his auto on
a gravel road near Crystal Lake.
He died shortly after he was
taken to Woodstock Hospital by
McHenry County sheriff's
police.

Cole, who lived at 703 Silver
Lake Rd., Cary, had called a
neighbor earlier Wednesday and
said he planned to take his life.
Police began a search and early
in the evening three boys told
authorities they had found a man
shot through the head in an auto
west of the intersection of Ill.
176 and Rt. 14.

Police found Cole in the front
seat, a .22 caliber rifle lying
across his body and a suicide
note on the seat beside him.

He was still alive but didn't
regain consciousness.

Cole's comic strip, Betsy and
Me, appears in The Sun-Times
and is distributed by The Chicago Sun-Times Syndicate. Cole
was also employed as a staff
cartoonist for Playboy magazine. Earlier in his career, he
had created Elastic Man, a
popular comic book for children.

He is survived by his widow,
Dorothy.

Funeral services are being
arranged.

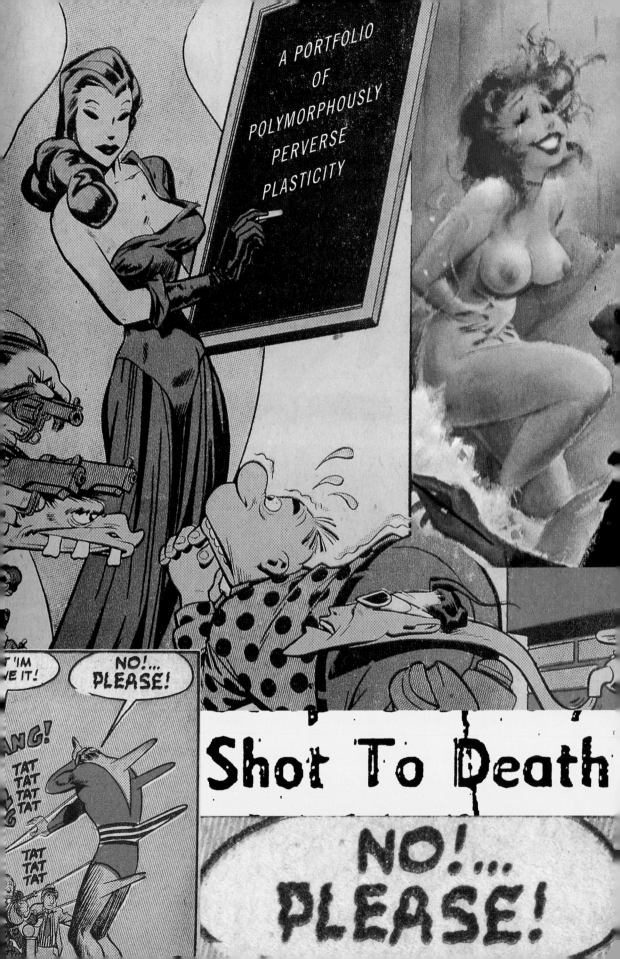

WHEN YOU READ THIS I SHALL BE DEAD
I CANNOT GO ON LIVING WITH MYSELF
& HURTING THOSE DEAR TO

WHAT I DO HAS NOTHING

NATURALLY.

HEY!
HEY!
HEY!
HEY!
HEY!
WHICH STRETCHES FARTHEST -- THE LONG ARM OF DEATH?... THE LONG ARM OF THE LAW?... OR THE LONG ARM OF PLASTIC MAN?
POLICE

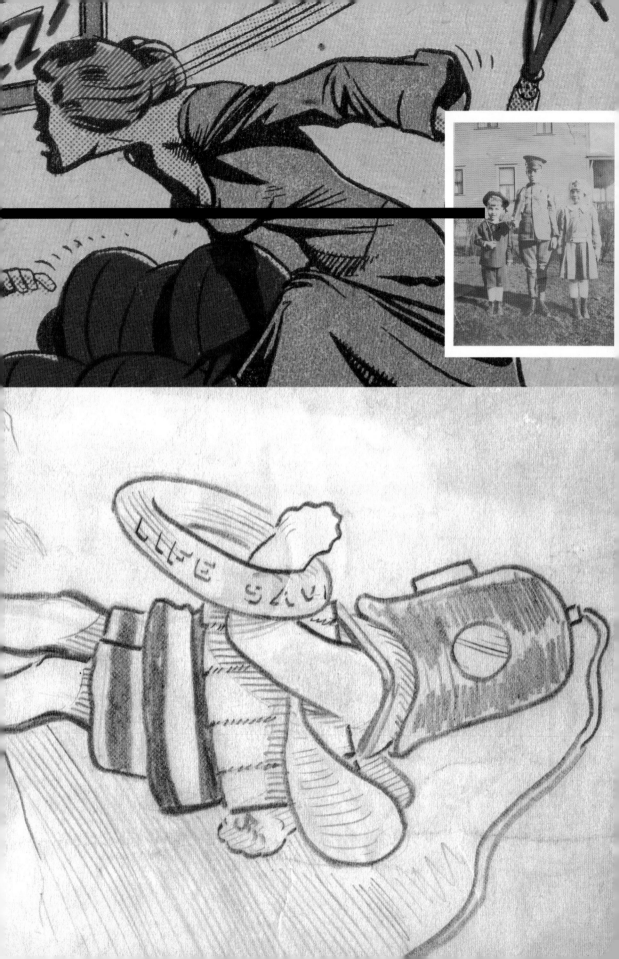

Nobody's Business.　By Jack Cole

"I said MOOSE hunting!"